SCHOOL
OF
LOVE

Planting a Church in the Shadow of Empire

ROGER D. JOSLIN

D1522997

Morehouse Publishing
NEW YORK

Morehouse Publishing, 19 East 34th Street, New York, NY 10016

Morehouse Publishing is an imprint of Church Publishing Incorporated.

www.churchpublishing.org

Cover design by Laurie Klein Westhafer

Typeset by Denise Hoff

Library of Congress Cataloging-in-Publication Data

Joslin, Roger D.

  School of love: planting a church in the shadow of empire / Roger D. Joslin.

    pages cm

  ISBN 978-0-8192-3193-2 (pbk.)—ISBN 978-0-8192-3194-9 (ebook)
1. Church development, New. 2. Church growth. 3. Church development, New—Episcopal Church. 4. Church growth—Episcopal Church. 5. Christianity and culture. I. Title.

  BV652.24.J67 2015

  283'.76713—dc23

               2015016949

Printed in the United States of America

To Cindee,
my tutor in the
School of Love

If you want to build a ship, don't drum up the people to gather wood, divide the work, and give orders. Instead, teach them to yearn for the vast and endless sea.

—Antoine de Saint-Exupery

Contents

Foreword

This book is not for the faint of heart. It is not for those that want to avoid the wilderness or the wild. It is not the latest "paint by numbers" approach to church growth or a strategy for success in congregational development. It is not a prescription for a new kind of church.

It is a love story. And there is a difference. As a bishop of the church I have whittled down all of the various ideas and strategies for growing a church to very few, but I think the first among them is really a question: do you love your people? If you can answer in the affirmative, I truly believe half the struggle is over, and the church, one way or the other, will thrive where you are. What Roger has done in this book is tell of the love he has for his people. Even more, he has cleared up another misconception we make along the way: "your people" are not only those who come to the church, but all those children of God who may never darken your door.

It is not that new, but the church grows, if not in numbers then in usefulness and perceived stature, when you go out the door and engage "your people." That is what this book is about, going into that wilderness of our neighborhood and finding "our people." That is the problem with a "welcoming" church. In fact, I have suggested we get out of that business, or at least not hold it up as our greatest value. It is far better to be an inviting church. Welcoming is good, we should do it, but it is a passive activity. Inviting is active. It takes confidence, and what you want to share has to be important

yes, be an inviting church not a welcoming church

enough and transformative enough in your own life to offer it to others. When you do, it becomes a gift.

Oh, by the way, Roger doesn't talk about it much in the book, but from 2006 to 2014, All Saints' went from one person, Roger, to 465 baptized members, an average Sunday attendance of 226, and pledges of over $280,000. Sounds like a going concern to me, and numbers I would take any day.

Roger tells the story of an important meeting he and I had, after we had worked together about a year. He recounts how I looked at him and asked, "Roger, how are we going to get you ordained?" To which he replied, "I don't know, how are we?" I am really glad we figured that out because he is that rare breed of priest, and deeper than that, Christian, who believes so strongly in a line I have to remind myself of daily; you can draw any line in the sand, and you will almost always find Jesus on the other side.

We live in a time of fear. Maybe that is not so different as in times past, but in our day the church may be one of the most fearful collectives going. That is truly sad, because that is not who we are or who the world needs us to be. Christianity has been on a mission to redesign itself when I think all we need to do is rediscover ourselves. This love story helps with that.

Roger adds an appendix, a list of 23 things he suggests you might try if you want to plant a church. This may be my only "beef" with the book. I like them all, but the most important one he has listed as number 16:

> Love the people, even if they aren't always lovable. If they know that you love them, they will forgive your inadequacies.

I might suggest he raise that either to number 1, or be the last, as a big finale! But its his book, not mine, and I can't argue with the results!

My favorite part of this book, most likely because it reminds me so much of the Roger I know, comes when he is describing the spring-fed creek on the property where the new church building will be erected. He rightly points out that it does not matter where a baptism takes place, it matters what it means, what it initiates, what it sets in motion. Or as he puts it so well

> What does matter is that we don't civilize things too much and that we don't refine the practice to the point that the wildness of the experience seeps away. We must always keep these sacramental practices sufficiently wild so that the Holy Spirit continues to be revealed to us.

Yes, indeed. Can I get an AMEN!

The Rt. Rev. Gregory H. Rickel
VIII Bishop of Olympia

Preface

I'm not sure if it was eager anticipation of the adventure ahead that rendered me oblivious to the leftward leaning of the needle on my truck's fuel gauge, or a failure to recognize how much wooded wilderness separated Bentonville from the rest of the world, but on my first trip to Northwest Arkansas I ran out of gas in the Boston Mountains, an hour shy of my destination. Literally, and metaphorically, I didn't know how far it was from my home in Austin, Texas, to Bentonville, Arkansas. I had a directive from the Bishop of Arkansas to plant a church in Bentonville, but I really didn't know how to start a church. I did possess something of an entrepreneurial spirit and I knew a little about launching a business. Along with the Diocesan Canon for Congregational Development, Dennis Campbell, I had attended a very evangelical church-planting "boot camp," but Episcopalians aren't generally recognized for their desire or their success in spreading the gospel by establishing churches on every street corner.

I did, of course, have something of a plan in mind. My initial approach to church planting involved little more than finding a variety of ways of becoming involved in the community and setting about making new friends. This rather simple arrangement gave me a chance to pass my days rather pleasantly and, in fact, proved to be an effective method of laying the groundwork from which a more substantial Christian community would eventually emerge.

It was only later, as I began to understand the unique character of the community in which I had landed and as the purpose motivating our growing band of Jesus followers began to unfold, that I had the knowledge and experience needed to conceptualize a church planting strategy. Initially, I had little more than a tactical approach to establishing a church. Over time, both strategically and theologically, the true nature of the mission unfolded. *School of Love* is the story of that unfolding.

It is obvious that if you want to grow a church you need to make contacts and establish relationships in the community. Some portion of your new friends and acquaintances will attend the meetings and gatherings and church services you eventually hold. Yet I discovered that there was a marked difference between the friendship-making style I adopted as a church planter and the way I had previously made friends. Most of my life I had been careful and highly selective about the people with whom I chose to spend time. As a church planter, I learned to let down the barriers to friendship I had previously erected. I opened myself up to encounters and relationships that I would have earlier shunned. I strived, not always successfully, to avoid asking myself whether a new acquaintance was a potential church member, whether we had anything in common, or even whether or not I liked them. Simple friendliness, practiced widely, without regard for age, race, class, sexual orientation, or religious persuasion, meant that diversity and acceptance of others who are different was built into the very fabric of All Saints' Bentonville.

Becoming involved in the community is a commonly accepted practice among successful church planters. I had been advised to choose activities that were natural and that I enjoyed. So, I was counseled, if I loved theater, I should join the local drama club, or if I had a child of little league age, I might coach baseball. That's useful guidance and might contribute to church growth, but such an approach to community involvement ignores the fact that the church is called to a higher purpose. The church planter sets the tone for the future church's relationship with the wider community by choosing activities that elevate the poor, reach out to the marginalized, contribute to social justice and, in the words of the Baptismal Covenant, "strive for justice and peace among all people, and respect the dignity of every human being." So it was that All Saints', from its inception, became known as a place that fed the hungry, offered relief to prisoners, provided hospitality to those not welcomed in other churches, and responded positively to the city's growing religious and cultural diversity.

I think of a school of love as a place where people can experience a widening of their circle of compassion. Tribalism and suspicion of "the other" is built into the human genetic makeup. Church, at its best, can be a place in which the barriers that separate us from one another are broken down, and we can realize that at our core we are all one in the spirit. As the circle of compassion within the church expands, there is the potential that the same sense of compassion can spill over into the larger community and a place where racism, homophobia, and fear of the other once reigned can move toward wider acceptance of those who are dissimilar.

This is the story of a church startup in a very specific context. However, most of what I have learned as a church planter is applicable to anyone who is interested in growing or revitalizing an existing church. There is plenty of discourse concerning "the dying church." I don't know anything about that. My experience tells me that when a gospel of compassion and acceptance is preached and practiced with passion, the church thrives. It might be that the essential components necessary for a successful church start-up or renewal can be reduced to just those two elements—a balanced combination of passion and compassion. It was a formula followed by Jesus in his first century school of love, and remains a sound practice today.

I would first like to thank Cindee Joslin, my companion in life and love, who faithfully watched and waited and wondered as both the church and the manuscript took shape. I must thank my dear mother, Lillian Joslin, now 96, who reminded me that I was called to ordained ministry as a child. I am grateful to my children,

Nathan Joslin and Lillian Conrad, whose love for me and for each other continue to fill me with great joy and hope for the future. I offer thanks to my son-in-law, Elliot Conrad, who, as a fine writer himself, understands the thrill of a completed manuscript.

I deeply appreciate the faculty and my fellow students at the Seminary of the Southwest, who inspired, challenged, and prepared me for this holy work. In particular I am grateful to the Very Rev. Cynthia Kittredge, my advisor at the Seminary of the Southwest, who stood by me when fainter hearts would have walked away. And every day I recall the example of the Rev. William Seth Adams, who, though his graceful sense of presence, taught me what it means to create "church."

I would like to thank the Very Rev. Steve Thomason, who was the first to ask if I had ever thought about serving as a priest in Arkansas. I am forever grateful to the Rt. Rev. Greg Rickel, who more than a decade ago saw something in me that made him think that I could plant a church. I must thank Ora Houston and the people of St. James' Episcopal Church, Austin, Texas, who schooled me, as a seminarian, in the practice of love and diversity. I offer thanks to my good friend, the Rev. Hunt Priest, who consoled me with every misstep and now rejoices with me at every success. And I offer gratitude to Greg Garrett, whose boundless creative energy continues to motivate and inspire me.

I must thank my two Arkansas bishops, the Rt. Rev. Larry Maze, who looked into my heart and who believed in me enough to offer me a job, and the Rt. Rev. Larry Benfield, who has continually supported and encouraged me and the mission of All Saints'. I remain in debt to the Rev. Dennis Campbell, who knows more about congregational development than anyone I know and who carefully shepherded me in the early days of the church plant. I am grateful for the friendship and example of the Rev. Lowell Grisham, whom I regard as the consummate priest. I would also like to thank the Rev. Doug Hester, whose insights into family systems theory kept me mindful of the challenge and the generational consequences of church planting.

Among the many All Saints' parishioners who helped make this book possible, I must recognize Chet Jechura, the initial reader of the manuscript and a talented editor, who quickly grasped what it meant to be enrolled in the School of Love. I extend thanks to Greg Warren, who with one foot planted in the corporate world and one planted in the church, provided a perspective no one else could offer. And I thank Sharon Orlopp, Chief Global Diversity Officer at Walmart, who repeatedly reminded me and the people of All Saints', "You have made a difference."

I extend my thanks to Richard Bass, my editor, who made me smile when he informed me that *"School of Love* is great" and then with his skillful hand made it a better book. I would also like to thank Church Publishing's Ryan Masteller and Jennifer Hackett for their capable assistance.

I will be forever grateful to the people of the Diocese of Arkansas, whose financial support and enthusiasm for the mission of All Saints' enabled and sustained our work. And finally, I present my heartfelt appreciation to the members of All Saints' Episcopal Church, Bentonville, who through their faithfulness to the cause of Christ created our beautiful school of love.

Introduction

How does one know when to celebrate? I once celebrated a marriage that should have been an occasion for mourning. And I can vividly recall my elation upon receiving a business loan that ended in economic disaster. I've seen joy turn to sorrow, and tears turn into laughter, so often that I've lost confidence in my talent for telling good news from bad. So it was that, at the close of a bitterly cold day in February 2015, only my lack of agility and trepidation over how the future might unfold enabled me to resist leaping high into the air and clicking my heels together. Three notable events occurred that day; they mark not the end of the story but a moment when the story of the creation of All Saints' Episcopal Church of Bentonville, Arkansas, has briefly paused so that an account can be shared.

Correspondence with a county sheriff seldom brings good tidings to the average citizen, but on this morning the news was excellent. An e-mail message from the Benton County sheriff assured me that he had signed a contract with the jail's food service supplier to provide hot meals to the prisoners under his charge. A seven-year struggle to remove the Benton County jail from the very short list of jails in the United States that serve only cold food to their prisoners had finally met with victory. It was the culmination of a process that began with my startling discovery upon arriving in Bentonville that, in the hometown of Wal-Mart Stores, Inc., the county sheriff couldn't find it in his heart, or in the county's

coffers, to feed its prisoners much of anything but cold, stale sandwiches. The events following my awareness of the prisoners' plight
led to a confrontation with a sheriff that almost ended in fisticuffs,
the eventual election of a more enlightened sheriff, a rallying of
our congregation around the idea of cooking the meals themselves,
preaching, teaching, articles in the local paper, a heated Facebook
exchange over a graphic depiction of the jail's typical meal of
bologna on white bread, a trip to the Arkansas State Capitol to meet
with the jail standards commission and copious conversations and
e-mail exchanges with the keepers of the jail. And so it was that
the parishioners of All Saints' savored the sweet taste of victory
and the county's most unfortunate citizens, barred from life's most
basic amenities, could at least taste the comfort of a hot meal.

On that same cold morning, Walmart announced that it would
immediately raise the hourly wage for their lowest-paid employees
from the federally mandated minimum of $7.25 an hour to $9.00 an
hour, and then to $10.00 an hour the following year. The announce-
ment was met with wide-ranging reactions. Labor groups found the
increases inadequate and gave credit for the rise in wages to the per-
sistence of workers and their allies. Economists noted that a more
healthy economy and a tightening job market naturally leads to an
increase in wages in order for companies to retain qualified workers
and maximize profitability. Explaining the decision, Walmart CEO
Doug McMillon said, "What's driving us is we want to create a
great store experience for customers and do that by investing in our
own people." The *New York Times* said the action "appears to be
an attempt to stem employee turnover and to respond to pressure
for higher wages from politicians, labor groups and employees."
There is no doubt that the move was prompted by many factors,
but I couldn't avoid smiling at the news and taking some satisfaction in the quiet role that All Saints' had played in the decision.
Walmart decision makers are less influenced by a *New York Times*
editorial than they are by a conversation on the Bentonville square,
a thoughtful sermon, a column written by a local clergyman, or the
well-placed comment of a compassionate and determined Walmart

associate. Behind the scenes, courageous Christians were having an influence.

In the evening of that same day, I drove across town to a meeting of the Benton County Interfaith Alliance. The Alliance is composed of representatives from Jewish, Muslim, Christian, Hindu, and Bahá'í traditions—a notable assemblage of religions anywhere, but an extraordinary gathering for a rural county in Arkansas. The world's largest retailer, with a presence on every major continent, was responsible for bringing their employees and their suppliers, along with their distinct faith traditions, to this unique community. A few months earlier, at an interfaith Thanksgiving celebration, Hindu, Muslim, and Christian clergy held a sacred scroll aloft while the rabbi knelt down and read from the Torah. It was a remarkable evening, and one that I could scarcely have imagined eight years ago at my first, and last, meeting of the Bentonville Ministerial Alliance. At that gathering the group voted to change its name to the Bentonville Christian Ministerial Alliance—in order to clearly differentiate themselves from other faiths and purposely exclude the variety of religions beginning to make their presence known in this corner of the Ozarks. And now, having completed the design development phase of a building program for a stirringly beautiful modernist church building, the people of All Saints' Episcopal Church find themselves in serious conversation with the Jewish congregation of Etz Chaim concerning the prospect of building an interfaith center, where both congregations can worship under the same roof. There is even the possibility that our Muslim brothers and sisters might join with us in the creation of a center where all three Abrahamic faiths could gather as one.

The likelihood that three major endeavors, on which our church has worked for years, could come to fruition on a single day seems remote. Yet despite its improbability, this moment in time provides a suitable platform from which to delve into the story of how we arrived at this juncture. As implausible as the triptych of events occurring on that single freezing February day seems to be, so were the fantastic series of events that unfolded in the eight years leading up to that day—occurrences that stretched and shaped an ordinary group of churchgoers into a people of God with a heart for justice and inclusion.

For the early Jesus followers living in Rome and the residents of the nations under their sway, the presence of an empire presented a decidedly mixed blessing. The *Pax Romana* offered peace with a steep price. Roman officials maintained order, but exacted crippling taxes and tribute from their subjects. Strict allegiance to the emperor was enforced with the weight of the Roman boot. The kingdom of God that Jesus proclaimed offered a different kind of peace, a kingdom based on compassion and justice, a kingdom that was not of Caesar. The presence of the Roman Empire was ubiquitous. The legions brought with them the culture, the customs, and the commerce of Rome and Rome's influence flavored every inch of the societies it touched.

Yet without Rome, Christianity could not have spread. The Roman network of all-weather roads connected disparate parts of the empire. Paul's missionary journeys followed those Roman roads. International trade and commerce brought with it the opportunity for a fluid exchange of ideas. It was in the international marketplace of Rome and its environs that Christianity eventually found a firm foothold and spread throughout the Empire.

Sometimes I imagine that planting a church in Bentonville feels a little like the early Jesus followers must have felt as they established the early church in the Roman Empire. Certainly Walmart possesses none of the military, political, and ideological muscle that characterized the power of the Romans, but Walmart's economic dominance is indisputable. In terms of revenue, Walmart is the world's largest company, the biggest private employer in the world, and the globe's largest retailer. It operates in twenty-six countries outside of the United States. If Walmart were a country, it would be the twenty-fifth largest economy in the world.

Just as the residents of Rome enjoyed the economic and cultural benefits of Roman citizenship, so the citizens of Bentonville take pleasure in the parks, trails, restaurants, good schools, and museums that would not exist in their community without the presence of Walmart. There is no small irony in the fact that Bentonville has a lovely town square that buzzes with retail activity throughout the year while stores lining the square in thousands of small towns across the United States lie vacant because shoppers flock to the Walmart on the edge of town.

The "Home Office," as Walmart's corporate headquarters is locally known, is not located in a glittering, multistory edifice. Visitors are surprised to find that the sprawling red brick building closely resembles a second-rate community college. Entering the windowless, warehouse-like interior, one finds acre upon acre of cubicles, stretching as far as the eye can see, where "associates," as Walmart employees are called, conduct business with the world. Only when the sun is very low on the horizon does the Home Office cast any physical shadow at all. Yet the presence of the Home Office is ubiquitous across the planet, and, most certainly, in this quintessential company town.

The journalist and novelist Tom Wolfe has explained why he chooses to show up on an assignment wearing his trademark white suit and two-tone shoes: "It is much more effective to arrive at any situation as a man from Mars than to fit in." Arriving in Bentonville, Arkansas, dressed entirely in black, apart from the white clerical collar around my neck, and holding a fresh mandate from the bishop to plant an Episcopal church here, I understood something of how the storied man from Mars might have felt. It wasn't long before I also realized that I too might be more effective if I avoided fitting in too neatly in Bentonville. Wearing a black suit and a white clerical collar seemed to help me keep an appropriate distance, but it also served as an entree into Arkansas culture.

Bentonville is a churchgoing kind of place, and a "man of the cloth" is immediately accorded some modicum of respect. Nonetheless, while you can't open your car door without hitting a preacher, it is rare on the streets of Bentonville to encounter a priest. The novelty of my presence worked to my advantage. From the beginning, I was noticed and curiosity often got the best of the residents. Often, I was asked, "What are you?" or "Are you a preacher or something?" But more often, the collar simply proved to be a conversation starter and allowed me to get a glimpse of the lives of those I encountered. In a larger sense, I eventually was included in the "conversation" the community had about what it was and where it was going. And it has proven to be a very interesting conversation, indeed.

With a population of a mere forty thousand, Bentonville is among the best known small towns in the United States. Its fame, or perhaps notoriety, is attributed to its status as the home of Walmart, the largest corporation in America. The commission I had received from the bishop was to start a church here. Dozens of churches had already sprung up in Bentonville—mainline churches, as well as many of a variety of evangelical flavors. The idea of starting an Episcopal church in Bentonville had been a topic of discussion within the Diocese of Arkansas for over a decade, but many wondered whether a decidedly liberal church could succeed within the conservative religious and political climate here.

The Episcopal Church, whose liturgical style of worship is deeply rooted in an ancient Christian tradition, has moved in a theologically progressive direction over the past century. The typical Episcopalian sees no conflict between science and the teachings of scripture, isn't a Biblical literalist, accepts the validity of other major world religions, values Christian practice over belief, rejects dogmatism, recognizes the importance of women in leadership roles in the church, fully accepts members of the LGBT community, favors same-sex marriage, and, more often than not, thinks a cocktail before dinner might not be a bad idea. Considering the conservative religious culture that is dominant here, it is easy to understand why one might question whether Bentonville was "fertile ground" for planting an Episcopal church.

On the first day of my arrival in Bentonville, I rented a garage apartment across the street from the local cemetery. After my Australian shepherd, Tyke, and I passed the interview with my new landlord, the landlord and I shook hands and I said, "Freddie, you are my best friend in Bentonville." Freddie was, in fact, the only person I knew in the entire county. However, Bentonville is a friendly place and my church planting strategy of making friends wherever I went proved to be a good one. I went everywhere. I showed up for music at "picking on the square" every Friday evening in downtown Bentonville. I attended city council and quorum court meetings. I went to Chamber of Commerce and Rotary Club events, fairs, concerts, lectures, plays, and even the Mule Jump at Pea Ridge.

During the first years of our mission, Bentonville still retained a distinctly small town atmosphere, but with a difference. To my surprise, I discovered that there were seven places to eat sushi, and most were good. My puzzlement at this phenomenon was eventually resolved as I realized how extensively Walmart employees traveled. It was not unusual for an Arkansawyer with a high school education to find herself traveling to China to purchase merchandise or flying to Africa or South America to coordinate the delivery of goods. These small town people often returned from their travels not just with a taste for exotic foods, but with new experiences and an expanded worldview.

Not long before I arrived, Walmart vendors recognized that if they were to do business with Walmart effectively, they would need to open offices nearby. Consequently, if you work for General Foods, Kraft, Kellogg, PepsiCo or one of the hundreds of other suppliers for Walmart, there is a good chance that, if you were going to advance your career, you would be expected to spend a few years working closely with your major customer. As a result, Benton

County began to grow rapidly and a new population of young, educated, and forward-thinking residents began to inhabit the area. Many found the slower pace of life, the mild climate, and the natural beauty of the surrounding Ozarks to be enticing enough to convince them to put down roots. As I was told many times by couples that had moved here from larger cities throughout the country, "This seems like a good place to raise a family."

It is not unusual to encounter a rich diversity of cultures in America's large cities, but in a small town like Bentonville it is astounding. Since Walmart does business internationally, citizens from every continent have made their home here. At the last count, I noticed seven Indian restaurants within a mile of the Walmart Home Office. The first Jewish synagogue started in a rural area of the U.S. in a half-century is here. There is a thriving mosque, and a new Hindu temple has been built. Extraordinarily, a Hmong community has settled nearby and their presence is made known at the downtown farmers' market on Saturday mornings. Perhaps most unexpected, the largest Marshallese community outside of the Marshall Islands has found its way to Northwest Arkansas.

The second largest employer in the area is Tyson Foods. Tyson employs thousands of workers, mostly Hispanic, in its meat processing plants here. Consequently, this corner of Arkansas has one of the fastest growing Hispanic communities in the country. Not long ago, I stood in line at the checkout stand at Walmart behind an Asian couple. After a few minutes, I realized that they were speaking in Spanish. Unable to resist hearing their story, I learned that they had moved to Bentonville from Chile, where there is a significant Asian population.

With rapid changes come challenges for a community, and great opportunities for me to be an agent for change emerged. Within weeks of my arrival, I realized just how responsive the community could be. A new trail that had been built in the north part of town was made of concrete. As a lifelong runner, I knew how damaging running on a concrete surface could be. After a couple of conversations with the city, a gravel path suddenly appeared alongside the concrete trail. In a climate accustomed to change, a variety of voices can be heard.

One of our early parishioners, Joe, is retired from a Walmart career. At one point, he was responsible for purchasing every shoe that Walmart bought from China. Long before Walmart paid close attention to the conditions of factories where their products were produced, Joe was asking factory owners about the lives of the workers, visiting their homes, and talking with them about how they were treated.

Before coming to Bentonville, I sometimes imagined that in order to get Walmart's attention, I might have to chain myself in protest to the giant Walmart sign outside the entrance to the Home Office. I'll still reserve that strategy as an option, but I have come to realize that I am in a unique position to have an impact on one of the most powerful corporations in the world, and by extension, on environmental concerns, employment practices, wages, and diversity issues by teaching and preaching a gospel of compassion, justice, and inclusion to a congregation of people who occupy positions of authority from which they can directly effect change within the organization.

It is hard to imagine that an ordinary Episcopal priest in a small town in Arkansas could have such an opportunity to make the world a better place. I am daily humbled and inspired by the example of faithful members of my congregation and by members of the larger community who are committed to the task of changing the world from the tiny vantage point of Bentonville.

CHAPTER 1

Preparing the Planter

Now the LORD said to Abram, "Go from your country and your kindred and your father's house to the land that I will show you."

—Genesis 12:1

"He doesn't have a lot of meat on his bones," my father confided to the preacher. I shivered as I cautiously stepped down the stairs leading to the baptistery and eased into the ill-heated and rapidly cooling pool. The water stood at waist-high for most of the baptismal candidates that were led into the water, but I was a slow-growing six-year-old and I rose on my tiptoes to keep my head above the surface. The white robe that Dad had slipped over my jeans and t-shirt encircled my skinny frame like a white tent held aloft by a single pole. In the water, the robe first mushroomed around me and then slowly drifted below the surface. The preacher, Brother Tennyson, was a family friend and a missionary to Brazil home on furlough. Baptist youth are raised on missionary lore and the adventures of missionaries from China and Africa filled my head and fueled my imagination. I assumed that Brother Tennyson had hiked out of the Brazilian rain forest and traveled to East Henderson Street Baptist Church, Cleburne, Texas, in order to baptize me.

Brother Tennyson placed his left hand behind my head and held my nose tightly shut with his right hand. "I baptize you in the name of the Father. . . " at that moment the sound was muffled, but enveloped in what I would now call the watery grave, I could still hear the distant sounding voice proclaim, "and of the Son, and of the Holy Ghost." The preacher lifted me above the water and nudged me in the direction from which I had come. Cold and dripping, I stepped up the stairs and received my father's embrace.

I don't recall whether I was selected to turn over the first spade of dirt because I was the youngest member of the church, or because I was the most recently baptized, or whether the fact that my father was chairman of the board of deacons came into play, but there I stood, side by side with a very elderly man, who smelled of the snuff that had long ago yellowed his teeth and now threatened to spill from his cheek. Brother Bruner was the oldest member of the congregation. Once again, I don't know if it was his age or his tenure as a baptized believer that made him the oldest member. I was probably the only one gathered on that dusty vacant lot beside the old church to ponder the question. Nevertheless, two shiny spades appeared and one was handed to me.

Baptists are short on ceremony. Too much ritual is regarded as "papist," but only the better-educated Presbyterians would use that word. The Baptists around me would simply regard with suspicion anything that seemed "too fancy." Still, the construction of a long-prayed-for new building called for some recognition and while there would be no candles, or incense, or solemn chants, a couple of useful new shovels could be appropriated to mark the occasion.

Dad prayed for God's blessing on their work and at the "Amen," he opened his eyes, looked at me, and said in a voice for everyone to hear, "As the youngest member ("Two weeks or six years?" I still wondered) of Henderson Street Baptist Church, Roger, would you commence the building of our new church by turning over the first spade of dirt?" I had done enough digging in our family garden to know that you placed a foot atop the heel of a spade in order to shove it into the ground, but my digging heretofore had largely been confined to freshly tilled soil. This was hardscrabble terrain, soil that hadn't been turned over since decades before when it was quickly exhausted by a few seasons of sharecropper-grown cotton.

And so, though I climbed atop the shovel with both feet and managed to balance myself and jump twice on the shovel like it was a pogo stick, I fell back to the ground and could see that, at most, a heaping tablespoon of dirt had been pried from the land's firm grasp. I could feel the disappointment in the murmurs of the grim faced deacons surrounding me. I looked up at their faces and wondered if I should take another shot at it or if there was only one opportunity to "turn over the first spade." I don't know if it was the biblical literalist streak that affected their decision-making or simply a recognition that my second attempt at pulling a substantial shovelful of dirt from the packed ground was unlikely to be more successful than the first, but Brother Stovall, respected owner of the local Chevrolet dealership, and a major contributor to the building fund, spoke for the group, "Well, I guess that's a start."

Church wasn't just something that happened on Sundays in my family. In addition to Sunday school and the worship service on Sunday morning, there was Training Union and more worship on Sunday evenings, Wednesday night worship, and an assortment of youth, choir, and visitation gatherings throughout the week. As a family, we often read the Bible and prayed together. The practice of religion permeated our lives and I took it seriously.

Weeklong summer church camp experiences were heavily laced with highly charged emotional appeals to be "saved" or to "dedicate your life to Christ." As an impressionable eleven-year-old,

I responded with wholehearted enthusiasm to a particular camp preacher's pleadings on a sultry summer evening for the souls of young boys to give "their all" to Jesus. To the recorded strains of "Just As I Am," I didn't hesitate to rise from my place on a wooden bench at the back of the outdoor pavilion, "walk the aisle," and tell the waiting preacher that God was calling me to "special service" in the church.

It would be easy for me to reflect on that summer evening with a cynicism resulting from fifty years of looking askance at the practice of evangelical Christianity. I recognize how easily youth can be led by strong emotional persuasion and I really had no clear idea of what "special service" in the church might mean. However, something in the "call" was real then and has remained with me. At the time, I had imagined that I might serve as a missionary to a village in Africa or in South America and spread the gospel to those who hadn't heard of Jesus. The call of adventure probably spoke to me more clearly than a call to serve God. Still, I am reminded by what my mother, upon learning that I was finally entering seminary decades later, remarked, "Well, son, you know God called you as a child."

In 1969, on the morning after I graduated from high school, I boarded a plane for the first time in my life and flew to Los Angeles. My intention was to spend a couple weeks visiting relatives and seeing the sights before returning to Texas. Southern California had other plans. Historically, "the summer of love" had occurred two years earlier in Haight Ashbury, but for a boy from Texas the summer of love was in full swing.

Tex Woolard, known as a hard drinker and locally famous for holding illegal cockfights in the woods behind his country house, had taken a job installing counterweight systems, which were used to raise and lower stage curtains, in theaters around the state. Tex, his wife, Reba, and their son Bill, a high school football teammate of mine, had rented a house on the beach not far away in Oceanside, California, so I paid them a visit. "Roger, you want a job?" Tex asked. I didn't hesitate for a moment, knowing that the apprentice steel workers' wages I would receive would be many times greater than the nickel a bale I could make hauling Coastal Bermuda hay back home.

I stayed with the Woolards most of the summer, working very hard every day until quitting time and then surfing on newly purchased long boards until sundown. After dark we roamed the streets of San Diego and Tijuana, narrowly avoiding serious trouble and discovering a world far different than the one we had known in a small Texas town.

On June 27, I turned eighteen years old and was required to register for the draft. Although the war in Vietnam had been raging for years, the war hadn't affected me personally and I hadn't seriously considered it. I had girls, football, and where I would go to college on my mind. And so, dutifully, without really giving it a thought, I took the day off from work, got on a bus, and went to San Diego to register.

My life changed on the bus ride home. Sitting behind me was a young man, only a couple of years older than me, who had just returned from a tour of duty in Vietnam. Post Traumatic Stress Disorder wasn't in my vocabulary at the time, nor was it part of the public conversation about returning Vietnam veterans, but clearly this soldier was suffering. I felt like I was the first person he had talked to since landing in California. It seemed that he couldn't stop himself from talking and was unable to understand how I might react to what he was telling me.

"I was a machine gunner," he said. "One afternoon, we were on patrol and we saw a bunch of gooks walking across a hillside. It was a funeral procession. Somebody had died and they were carrying the coffin to bury it, I guess. And so, we set up the machine gun and wiped them out. All of them . . . men, women and little kids. Everybody was dead. We killed them all. Hey, you want to see my ear collection?" Without waiting for my reply, the war-crazed kid unfastened the top button of his shirt and lifted the necklace from his chest. Maybe a half-dozen gristled human ears, each pierced with a jagged hole large enough to allow a frayed cord to penetrate the flesh, were arrayed and kept separate from one another by a crudely tied knot. The kid grinned widely and said, "What do you think?"

I didn't answer him but what I thought was that the people and the institutions that I had trusted had lied to me. At that moment, I realized that the world was not as it seemed. The world presented by my country, my church, and my family had been a lie and, now, my eyes were opened to that lie. My innocence was lost and I began to question what I had been taught.

The literalist approach to the Bible, accepted by the Baptist church in which I was reared, was one of the earliest fatalities to my newly surfaced questioning nature. I could no longer square the creation stories in Genesis with an understanding of evolutionary biology. My fundamentalist upbringing provided me with no way of understanding how scripture could be valued if it weren't literally true. Thus began my drift away from the church.

The Vietnam era draft lottery was first held in 1969 and the lottery number I drew was low: sixty-four. As long as I stayed in school, my student deferment would keep me out of the military. However, it was easy for me to see that while white, middle class kids like me could stay out of the military by remaining in school, the war was being fought by minorities and the poor. This seemed wrong, so I naïvely decided to take a moral stance by applying for conscientious objector status. The process involved much soul searching and the solicitation of letters written on my behalf from church leaders and family members. I quickly learned that while I had accepted Jesus's notions of peace and love and taken them quite seriously, my church had no difficulty reconciling support for a violent Asian war with Jesus's teachings concerning peace. The church was not supportive of my antiwar stance and so I moved even further away from the institution.

Throughout college, my opposition to the war in Vietnam and war in general began to take shape. After graduation and a year of travel, I decided to enter graduate school in the Department of Government at the University of Texas, with the intention of focusing on peace research. I completed my master's degree and eventually went to the University of Sussex in Brighton, England, to continue work in the field of conflict resolution. Eventually, I became disenchanted with the endeavor, concluding that the academic approach to the study of war and peace I was pursuing was unlikely to be fruitful. I was unaware of it then, but the peace I so fervently sought could only be found by first finding peace within myself.

After years of study and archival research in the British Public Records Office, I longed to see the result of my labor at the end of the day. I returned to the United States and, after a while, found that working with my hands in a cabinet shop gave me a great deal of satisfaction. The work was pleasing enough that, in one form or another, woodworking provided me with a livelihood for the next twenty years. I had discovered that I liked to build things. I worked on large and small projects alike, focusing primarily on premium grade architectural millwork. I succeeded and failed, ran my own company, and managed projects for others.

Peace and happiness remained an elusive goal and the marriage to my high school sweetheart was troubled. Church played no role in my life, but the remnant of a prayer remained after I closed my eyes at the end of each day: "God, show me your will for my life." A decade later, I was adrift. An overly ambitious business plan that had been foolishly undertaken in a faltering economy left me in bankruptcy. Divorce soon followed. I didn't know where to turn, but God turned toward me.

I remember reading an article in an issue of *Harper's* magazine about an English professor at Yale who had spent some time on retreat at Gethsemane, the Trappist monastery where Thomas Merton resided. I had known of Merton from my days in the antiwar movement. Merton was an outspoken critic of the war and found common ground with monks and holy men and women from religions outside Christianity. I had not been exposed to the deeply contemplative side of Merton; I only knew the public face. In the article, Merton was quoted as saying, "Prayer is the desire to pray."

At that moment, I realized that I badly needed to pray. And I understood Merton to mean that it wasn't necessary for me to learn how to pray. Possessing a desire to pray meant that I was already praying. I felt a profound feeling of relief wash over me. That small taste of communion with God was sufficient to launch me on an intense period devoted to the study and practice of contemplative prayer and meditation. Long periods of time spent "praying without words" eventually allowed me to open again to the experience of "praying with words" and a willingness to re-engage with church.

Knowing that I wouldn't feel at home in the church of my youth, a priest friend suggested that I visit a few Episcopal churches. In the Episcopal Church, I found an openness to intellectual and theological inquiry, an absence of dogmatism, a wide-ranging acceptance of people of different beliefs, classes, cultures, and sexual orientations. I found the practice of ancient rituals to be deeply compelling and I discovered beauty as a pathway to God. Attending a Christian education class at one church, I found that my thesis advisor from the University of Texas was in attendance and he was asking questions about the nature of God that would have gotten him thrown out of fundamentalist churches. I didn't know church could be this way and I was hooked. For the next decade, I became a very active layperson in the church and continued on a path of serious spiritual inquiry that involved reading, praying, taking classes, and attending retreats.

The Call

Jesus said, "Follow me and I will make you fish for people." And Simon Peter, his brother Andrew, and the sons of Zebedee, James and John, immediately left their nets and their boats and they followed Jesus. I love call stories. They describe an instant when things change dramatically, the moment of embarkation on a great adventure. This call to adventure is described by Joseph Campbell as a moment in which "destiny has summoned the hero and transferred his spiritual center of gravity to a zone unknown."

I'm not alone in my fascination with call stories. Across generations, many have responded to the story of J.R.R. Tolkien's *The Fellowship of the Ring*, where Frodo Baggins is summoned by the wizard Gandalf to leave behind his comfortable and contented Hobbit existence and embark on a most dangerous quest. In the science fiction world of the film *The Matrix*, millions of movie fans have been held spellbound by the adventures of Neo, who is summoned by Morpheus, a man who reveals to him that he is about to change the world. Recently, I heard Clarence Jones, an African American attorney who helped draft the "I Have a Dream" speech and played a pivotal role in the civil rights movement, describe how he had at first declined to leave behind his comfortable and successful California law practice and refused Dr. King's invitation to join him in Alabama. Later, hearing a sermon given before a large crowd, Clarence Jones couldn't resist Dr. King's personally directed invitation to join the movement. And his life and the lives of future generations of black and white Americans were forever changed. But the real reason I am taken with call stories is that I have one. My mother would tell you that I was called to ordained ministry as a child, but unlike Frodo Baggins, Neo, or Dr. King's attorney, it took me half a lifetime to respond to the call.

The call finally became irresistible in the Southern Rockies of Northern New Mexico, in a collection of mountains known as the Sangre de Cristo, "the blood of Christ." I had hiked there many times, usually early in the spring when the snows were melting, in order to find the solitude that I craved. On my way to the various trailheads, just north of the town of Pecos, I always passed by a Benedictine monastery and wondered about the monks inside. Before leaving my home in Austin, I called the monastery and the voice that answered, which belonged to Father Bob, was so warm and so welcoming that I decided instead of camping out in the mountains I would accept his invitation and stay with the monks.

During my visit, I prayed "the Hours" with the monastic community, shared meals, helped clean up, and did a few minor repairs to the monastery. I also talked with the monks. In particular,

I talked with a portly Irish monk named Brother Patrick. Brother Patrick, almost as wide as he was tall, and wearing the white cassock characteristic of the Olivetan order to which he belonged, closely resembled a large, fluffy marshmallow. We talked and we laughed while sitting on lawn chairs in the shadow of the Rockies. He jokingly held me, as a representative of the Anglican Communion, personally responsible for Henry VIII's sixteenth-century sacking and looting of Britain's Roman Catholic monasteries. One afternoon, after spending a few days in conversation, Brother Patrick said, "Roger, you need to be an Episcopal priest." And for the first time, I hesitated just for an instant before offering my usual litany of reasons why such a proposition was preposterous. I told him how I was too old, divorced, and too engaged in fatherhood and the business world to even consider the possibility of priesthood.

Later that day, I went for a run in the mountains. I crossed the footbridge arching over the headwaters of the trickling Pecos River behind the monastery and encountered a network of trails, abandoned logging roads, and animal paths crisscrossing the wilderness. I had only run a few miles when I spotted a lean, honey-colored mountain lion slowly crossing the path a few yards in front of me. I stopped in my tracks, expecting her to either leap upon me or run away. Instead, she turned and looked in my direction, holding my gaze in hers for an eternal moment. And then, having made it clear that this was her path and not mine, she turned and slowly ambled away.

When it was clear that she had moved on, I proceeded with my run, but the confusing array of dirt roads and trails made me wonder if I could find my way back, so I determined that I should mark the trail. At every uncertain intersection, I took two sticks and crossed them and laid them on the path so that one of the broken sticks pointed in the direction that would lead me home. I ran for countless miles, lightheaded from breathing the thin mountain air yet filled with the ecstasy of an intimate encounter with the majesty of God's created world that was endlessly arrayed before me. Finally growing tired, I turned around and began to retrace my steps. At the first intersection, I discovered that in marking the designated path, I had not simply placed one stick atop another, but I had created a cross. And upon my arrival at every intersection on my return journey, I discovered a single cross, pointing my way home.

After dinner that evening, as I sat in my simple monk's cell, I heard a knock at the door. I opened it and saw my friend Brother Patrick standing outside. "I have something for you," he said. In his hand was a small cardboard box, with a rubber band wrapped around it. "I want you to stand in front of the mirror and close your eyes." Obediently, I stood at the sink. Not so obediently, I watched in the mirror's reflection as Brother Patrick unbound the box and retrieved an object I couldn't quite make out from the tissue paper inside. I closed my eyes. When I opened them, Brother Patrick was standing behind me and I watched as he wrapped a clerical collar around my neck. In his simple wisdom, Brother Patrick understood that it wasn't enough that I be called, but that I must be shown. We are all called to the hero's quest, to the grand adventure that Jesus offers, however it is revealed to us through the Brother Patricks, the lions, or even the crosses that inhabit our lives.

And as a people, we are the inhabitants of the Land of Zebulon, the Land of Naphtali, on the road by the sea. And as citizens of that kingdom, we are people who have sat in darkness and have witnessed a great light. We are a people called to respond to the dawning of the light, for the kingdom of heaven has drawn near to us. When we answer the call, we are granted a glimpse of that kingdom. I'd like to say that the time from that epiphanous moment in New Mexico to the day I was ordained a deacon and sent by the bishop to start a church in Bentonville could be described as an easy, unencumbered journey. But that would be far from the truth. I was compelled, like the wise men, to take the journey home by another road.

The ordination process in the Episcopal Church is an arduous path, but the call to priesthood echoed loudly in my ears. At first, things went swimmingly. I had the support of my parish priest and a discernment committee. The vestry of my home parish unanimously recommended me. After the last of a series of meetings with the Commission on Ministry in the Diocese of Texas, the chairman hugged me and told me that the commission had never more enthusiastically supported a candidate. Then I was sent to see the bishop. A few days after a brief meeting with him, I received a letter of rejection that read: "Sometimes I accept candidates who are older, but they are generally more successful in business." It was one of the darkest days of my life, but something compelled me to "follow the star that I had seen at its rising" and I persisted. Shortly after receiving the rejection letter, I began my studies at The Episcopal Seminary of the Southwest in Austin without a sponsoring diocese.

And then, another epiphany occurred. Before my first week at seminary my entering class took a retreat together. I was fortuitously assigned to room with Steve Thomason, then a postulant from the Diocese of Arkansas and now dean of Saint Mark's Cathedral in Seattle. On our third day together, after learning that I wasn't attached to a diocese, Steve asked, "Have you ever thought of coming to Arkansas?"

My answer: "No, never."

"It might be a possibility," he said.

I continued with seminary, stretching my studies over four years instead of the usual three because I was also working full-time. Like all seminarians, I was also assigned to serve at a local parish. My assignment was St. James' Episcopal Church, and the rector was the Rev. Greg Rickel, who, as it turns out, was originally from Arkansas. After working with Greg for a year, I sat down with him for coffee one morning and he said, "Roger, how are we going to get you ordained?"

"I don't know, how are we?" I replied. The eastern star began to rise above the horizon.

Greg wrote a letter on my behalf to the Rt. Rev. Larry Maze, then bishop of Arkansas, telling him of an older than average seminarian, with more than a few scars from life, who possessed an entrepreneurial bent that might be useful in the Diocese of Arkansas.

Soon, I met Bishop Maze, a kindred spirit who was willing to take a gamble on me. And the star rose a little higher in the east.

For a year, I met with yet another Commission on Ministry, which I think finally concluded that I had been damaged and healed in ways that might have taught me enough about compassion to properly serve people. Then there were background checks, physical examinations, and interviews with psychiatrists, psychologists, and lawyers. Through it all, the star continued to rise. Finally, a battery of psychological tests revealed that I just might be crazy enough to take on the task of planting a church in Bentonville. And the star moved closer to a point in the sky above the Ozarks.

At long last, I was ordained. The bishop directed me to go to Benton County to plant a progressive church, and I could see by then that the star that I had noticed at its rising had already stopped over Bentonville. And it was in Bentonville that the birth of All Saints' Episcopal Church was about to take place. I don't know if the average All Saints' parishioner would describe the moment or the series of events that led them to participate in the birthing of this church as an epiphany. It is more likely that a person came to All Saints' at a friend's suggestion than being led by a bright beam of light shining from a star.

Many parishioners will attest that this church is a revelation of what could be the future of Bentonville, and many have been attracted to All Saints' because they are not welcome anywhere else. Our practice of radical hospitality encouraged progressive members of the community to be part of what we are creating. Others discovered the church by attending one of our public events or by learning of our service to the community. Practically speaking, some folks were raised in the United Methodist Church, married a Roman Catholic, and found the Episcopal Church to be a good compromise.

Whatever kind of star guided them here, I always like for people to entertain the idea that their arrival at All Saints' may be as much of an epiphany for them as the wise men's own visit to Bethlehem. The wise men were overwhelmed with joy at the realization that they were present at the birth of something remarkable.

The members of All Saints' are also witnesses to the birth of a miracle. And just as the wise men could not have known that this child in a manger would one day be called Emmanuel, "God with us," so it is impossible for us to know what great things God has in store for the mission of All Saints' or other progressive church plants like it. All the founding families of All Saints' are called to follow the star and see where it leads. And so are you. Welcome to the adventure.

Looking Like the Kingdom

On the day of Epiphany, Christians around the world commemorate the appearance of a star "rising in the east" and guiding a group of wise men, who followed the star until it stopped over the place where the child Jesus was discovered with his mother, Mary. They knelt before Jesus and presented him gifts of gold, frankincense, and myrrh. We recognize in the Epiphany the manifestation of the divine nature of Jesus to the Gentiles as represented by the wise men from the east. Outside the context of church, epiphany denotes an unexpected manifestation of the essence or meaning of something; it is a sudden intuitive realization very much like the wise men's impulsive decision to drop everything and follow a star in the night sky.

During the years I attended seminary in Austin, Texas, I was assigned to work at St. James' Episcopal Church. The church was historically black. From its founding in 1941 until the early 1980s, the congregation remained almost entirely African American. The change began slowly. Austin has a vibrant and diverse music scene, with perhaps more live music than any other city in the country. Austin City Limits brought Austin music to the national consciousness. Aware of the importance of music, the people of St. James' launched an annual event, a weekend of music, called "Jazz at St. James'." They held concerts on Friday and Saturday nights, music workshops for children on Saturday, and a Jazz Mass on Sunday.

White folks showed up for the music, looked around and thought, "Wow, this is a cool place." And many stayed, drawn by the music and the deep sense of spirituality that the church had to offer. All kinds of people began to notice that the Holy Spirit was operating there in a way that demanded attention. The congregation was so friendly and welcoming that sometimes the passing of the peace could last longer than the sermon. In combination with the beauty of the ancient liturgy, a sense of timelessness prevailed in worship. The openness of the church to white and black alike attracted members of the gay and lesbian community, who also felt at home there. It wasn't long before St. James' began holding a Spanish mass as well.

The epiphany came to me one Sunday when I stood at the altar and looked out over the sea of people that comprised the All Saints' congregation. They were rich, poor, black, white, brown, gay, and straight. I suddenly realized that this is what the kingdom of God looks like. It was an epiphany not unlike the appearance of these three foreign magicians from the east to the Christ Child. The epiphany was a sign that Christ's coming wasn't just meant for a tiny Semitic tribe of wanderers, but that the entire world might be saved. Because of the international commerce of Walmart, it is a good fortune in Northwest Arkansas to have travelers from the east, west, north, and south. Like the wise men, these newcomers arrive bearing the gifts of their culture, their language, and their heritage. It is a real privilege, like that of the Christ Child, to receive these gifts from foreign lands and to share in the overwhelming joy of the wise men.

I was ordained to the priesthood in December 2006. It was one of those times when the presence of the Holy Spirit was unmistakable. There is a moment in the ordination service when all clergy who are present are asked to come forward and place their hands on the ordinand. The ritual is part of the tradition of apostolic succession, the belief that there is a continual link between St. Peter and all the priests that have succeeded him. In my naïveté before the ordination, I thought this laying on of hands sounded like a nice idea and a beautiful gesture, a ceremonial linking together of my brother and sister priests. How foolish I was! At the consecration, while I knelt in front of Bishop Maze and listened to him say, "Therefore, Father, through Jesus Christ your Son, give your Holy Spirit to Roger. . . ," I became aware at that very moment of the heaviness of the hands that were pressing down hard on my head and shoulders. It was as if I was bearing the weight of two thousand years of Christianity. The hands of generation upon generation of priests were making me a priest, quite literally. My breath went out of my body as all those hands that were pushing down began to ground me. They pushed me toward the earth, the very place where ministry happens.

Part of the process of my becoming a priest in the Diocese of Arkansas involved sponsorship by a church within the diocese. The bishop selected St. Margaret's in Little Rock to be my sponsoring parish, so in my final seminary year I made frequent trips from Austin to West Little Rock in order to get to know the clergy, vestry, and members of the community. It was my first trip to St. Margaret's and the Gospel reading for the day was the parable of the evil tenants as told by Luke. This is a parable that is traditionally interpreted to be a condemnation of religious leaders who had rejected Jesus. The preacher that Sunday, the Rev. Joanna Siebert, began the sermon with a parable of her own—the parable of the absentee Texas landlord. I recall her retelling of the parable going something like this:

> A wealthy rancher from Texas, wearing a black Stetson hat and boots, traveled to Arkansas and bought a thousand acres of river bottom land. He hired local tenant farmers from Searcy to till the soil and plant the crops and bring in the harvest. They struck a deal that allowed the tenants to keep a portion of the profits. With a penetrating look into the tenants' eyes and a firm handshake to seal the deal, the wealthy Texas landowner promised to return the

following year. Then, he climbed into his very big, black pickup truck, which had a gun rack adorning the rear window and tires so big that you needed a stepladder to climb aboard. The rancher then drove back to Texas. The tenants didn't hear a word from him until about a year later, when they looked up from their work in the fields and saw the black truck speeding down the dirt road leading to their shack, a cloud of dark dust trailing after him. He climbed down from his truck, muttered a greeting, and demanded his share of the profits. The tenants explained that the rain hadn't fallen, the soil was worn, and they had had a hailstorm that destroyed most of the harvest. The Texan said, "I'll see you next year," and he climbed back in the black truck and sped away. He returned the following year, demanded his money, and listened to another tale of bad weather and poor soil. The third year, the rich Texan returned and was greeted with the news that the weather and the soil again hadn't cooperated and the harvest was very poor indeed. So the rich Texan angrily threw the tenant farmers from the land, demanding that they and their families leave that very afternoon.

I wasn't a wealthy landowner and I certainly wasn't wearing a black hat and boots, which would look kind of funny poking out of the bottom of my alb. But I was from Texas and I did drive a rather large pickup, so I began to squirm a bit in my upright chair behind the lectern. I began to wonder just how hospitable this new land of Arkansas was going to be for this particular Texan. As it turned out, the people of Arkansas, and in particular the parishioners at St. Margaret's, were very hospitable to a University of Texas alum like me. What I came to understand was that the preacher that morning was "preaching against the grain." She was attempting to reveal something in the gospel that would be missed if the scripture were only read superficially and if the most commonplace, the generally accepted interpretation, were always preached. It's a practice I often adopt myself, and not just because I'm a little contrarian. It's a way of preaching the parables that Kirk Hadaway, author of *Behold I Do a New Thing: Creating Communities of Faith,* says involves a tearing down of illusions, a disruption, a shattering of the familiar: "a verbal hand grenade thrown by Jesus, to blow up our settled, taken for granted worlds."

While I had no intention of throwing verbal hand grenades upon my arrival in Bentonville, I was fairly certain that my presence in this small town would be unsettling to many of its residents. Proclaiming the gospel in the home of one of the world's most powerful corporations is necessarily disruptive.

CHAPTER 2

Gathering the People

Then Amos answered Amaziah, "I am no prophet, nor a prophet's son; but a herdsman, and a dresser of sycamore trees."

—Amos 7:14

I n each of the parables from Matthew's Gospel, Jesus relies on the familiar and everyday activity of peasant life in order to tell his story. Examples include the farmer planting a small seed that grows into a great tree, the woman using yeast to bake bread, the merchant who finds a valuable pearl, and fishermen catching fish of every kind. And then, in asking the disciples if they understood the parables, Jesus makes the point that he is using something old from the familiar everyday activities of peasant life to show them a very different way of being in the world, to bring out of his treasure "what is new and what is old."

That is part of what progressive church plants like All Saints' have to offer: both the old and the new, combining an ancient liturgy with a theological understanding that speaks to contemporary hearts and minds. By weaving the two worlds together, we can find an understanding of the old in a way that is transformational, which doesn't merely reinforce old self-congratulatory ways of knowing.

But it is more than just a blending of theology and liturgy. We are in the business of finding treasure anew. We must seek, not simply to grasp God's transforming purpose for us, but to be grasped by that purpose ourselves. We seek not just an understanding of what God is up to in the world, but personal transformation as well. It is easy and tempting to regard parables as tidy moral lessons applicable in all times and in all places. But without a particular context, they are virtually meaningless.

Bentonville is home to what is perhaps the most powerful corporation in the world. Materialism is the order of the day. Great wealth and financial struggle exist side by side. Racism and homophobia are ugly realities. This is a church-going community, but one that is dominated by biblical literalism. Here, in the midst of all of the above, is All Saints', an upstart of a church that boldly proclaims that all God's children are welcome just as they were created and dares to suggest that God wants us to use our brains as well as the Bible to understand what God is saying to us. This is a community that cares about the environment and seeks justice for all creation. It is a parish that seeks social change and risks being transformed in the process.

I arrived in Bentonville driving my pickup and towing a small U-Haul trailer containing virtually everything I owned. I spent my first night in town at the La Quinta Inn, a pet-friendly place that allowed my old dog, Tyke, to sleep in my room beside the bed. I spent most of the next day looking for a place to live. I found a small garage apartment on Southwest "F" Street, across the street from the cemetery, with a kitchen window that overlooked the grave of Bentonville's most famous resident, Sam Walton.

It was a small beginning, a mustard seed of a beginning. And from that tiny seed has grown what I think has become a shrub capable of providing much shelter for the birds of the air. From early on, many people have been involved in the nurturing and tending of this shrub of a church. But if the potential of All Saints' Episcopal Church is to be realized, if it is to grow into the tree that it is meant to be and if it is to truly be able to provide shelter and feed all God's children, then every member of the church must risk being transformed in the process.

To ensure that every person who enters the doors of All Saints' is welcomed in a way that assures them that they have found a home, we have created what we call "Hospitality Guilds." The guilds are meant to provide the kind of sanctuary that the ancient Benedictine monasteries of Europe once offered travelers: greetings, prayers, and food. Members of each of the six guilds share the responsibility for ensuring that every visitor to All Saints' feels welcome. On any given Sunday, each guild prepares and serves food, brings up the oblations of bread and wine during communion, and makes sure that no one sits alone during coffee hour. Many All Saints' parishioners have responded to my request that they be part of these guilds. Hospitality is the lifeblood of a growing church. Offering hospitality of this sort provides a way of participating in a new parable, a new way of envisioning the kingdom of heaven.

Buried in those cryptic, brief, sayings concerning mustard seeds, yeast, buried treasures, and pearls of great price resides transformational wisdom. Each parable provides a clue, a way of grasping just what it is that God is up to in this place. But if we are to be grasped ourselves, if we are willing to be changed and made anew, we must enter into the parable and become part of the story. That is God's invitation for each of us.

Radical Hospitality

While the time was right to start a church in Bentonville, the growth we have achieved has largely been due to the message we have proclaimed. The message is a simple one: "Whether you are black, white, brown, rich, poor, gay, or straight, you are welcome at All Saints' Episcopal Church." This welcome is a statement of radical hospitality. We accept people as they are. And this is just what Jesus did. He reached out to the people on the margins, to those that society found unacceptable. Jesus embraced the prostitutes, the tax collectors, and the poor. It is easy to love people who are just like ourselves, but Jesus asks us to do more. Jesus asks us to love people who are different from us. Progressive church plants must be sure to spread this message.

Fortunately, a reporter for the *Benton County Daily Record* heard our message at All Saints', and found it unusual enough to write a story about. The response was amazing. I am still answering the many inquiries that resulted from the newspaper article describing our notion of "radical hospitality." For one reason or another, the people who felt that the existing churches had rejected them have reached out to us and have since found a home at All Saints'. Not everyone who lives in a community feels completely at ease with the values of the dominant culture.

Attitudes toward the presence of Walmart and Walmart corporate policy vary widely among Bentonville residents. Many people have come to the Bentonville area from other parts of the United States and from many other parts of the world. Not all have settled in easily. Many members of the gay and lesbian community have been rejected by society-at-large and long to be accepted by a church. Bentonville likes to pretend that the poor don't exist; meanwhile, the poor cry out to be acknowledged as significant even when they don't share in the economic abundance of an affluent society. And churches have wounded other people; a young woman named Sarah told me of the humiliation she still feels, a decade after a fundamentalist preacher compelled her, at fifteen years old, to stand before the congregation of her church and apologize for being unmarried and pregnant. Still others have discovered that the mainstream churches they had been a part of for many years have shifted theologically to the right and left them behind.

After a few weeks in Bentonville, I was growing comfortable with the mantra I heard myself saying over and over to those that

I met, "We are creating a church where all are welcome: whether you are black, white, brown, rich, poor, gay, or straight." Then one afternoon, a simple inquiry challenged me to expand this notion of inclusion. The question was posed to me, "What do you know about Alcoholics Anonymous?" My admission that I knew relatively little resulted in an invitation to attend a specially constructed AA and Al-Anon meeting, which was designed for the precise purpose of acquainting me with the experience of alcoholics and the church.

We met at a home on the shores of one of Bella Vista's lakes. The group shared a delicious potluck dinner with me and then I listened to one painful story after another of people who no longer felt that they had a home in the church. These are people for whom church had once been a very important part of their lives. The church, however, had failed them. The church had failed to provide them with an alternative to the world that was as compelling as the allure of drugs and alcohol. In seeking to escape from this world, they had found that the senses could be dulled and that the thirst for God could be, at least temporarily, quenched by alcohol.

After following, and then with much struggle rejecting, the destructive path of addiction, these people had found wholeness through the community support of fellow AA members and a submission to a higher power. For these people, the world of spirit that Jesus offered to his disciples was not an abstraction. Rather, it was the clear alternative of sobriety, a chance to awaken to a new life. But even though they were now sober, most could find no home in the church. They missed the music, singing in the choir, the feeling of being in church, the comfort of hearing prayers that they had known since childhood, and the smell of incense. However, few had found church to be the transforming medium that they had found through AA. The church had not offered them life. Instead, the church they knew offered condemnation, exclusion, and a narrow literalist conception of a God that they had trouble reconciling with the more inclusive and broader idea of a "higher power" to which they had learned to submit control through their participation in AA.

They felt at home in their AA meetings. In churches, they imagined that they would be about as welcome as some old drunk stumbling into the worship services, sinking into the back pew, stinking of urine and cheap whiskey. Maybe it's all crazy talk, this idea of creating a church where all are welcome, black, white, brown, rich, poor, gay, or straight and where the addict and the alcoholic are equally offered the transforming power of Jesus's love. Maybe it's as crazy as the troubling idea that Jesus's flesh is true food and Jesus's blood is true drink. But if we who strive to be Christ's church don't offer a "welcome home" to those at the margins of society, then to whom can they go?

Freedom Fries

One morning, I was sitting alone at one of the plastic booths at the Station Café, the greasy hamburger joint on the square, two doors down from the original Walton's Five and Dime store. It may be the last restaurant in the country to still hold the French in such low regard for their unwillingness to join George W. Bush in his Iraqi escapade that they persist in calling their fried potatoes "Freedom Fries."

Cecil, the owner, was lecturing one of his young employees on the value of hard work and punctuality, qualities he urged the young man to acquire quickly so that he could "get ahead in this world" or at least keep his job flipping burgers. A teenaged waitress, more adept at avoiding the owner's morning counsel, busied herself arranging cutlery and keeping my teacup filled and hot. She commented on the theology book I was reading, then on the cold biting wind outside, and finally garnered the courage to ask the question that had puzzled her since I had walked in. "What are you?" she asked. The clerical collar that I wear is a calling card of sorts, often giving me the chance to talk with folks about their spiritual journey and the work that is being done at All Saints'.

After telling her about myself another question naturally followed: "So. . . Where is your church?" I happily told her. I usually give the address and maybe some directions to people who inquire about the location of All Saints'. However, what I really want to add is "Come and see." Because the question I want to answer isn't just "Where are you located?" but "Where do you abide? What are you about? Who are you people? And is this a place where I can be loved?"

In John's Gospel, Jesus uses the word "abide" repeatedly: "Abide in me as I abide in you. . . . As the Father has loved me, so I have loved you; abide in my love" (John 15:9). When Jesus offered his disciples an invitation to "come and see," he was asking them to take the first step in a journey of discovering what it means to be truly loved, to find a love that is abiding and enduring. And after spending an afternoon with Jesus, Andrew left to tell his brother Simon, "We have found the Messiah." It's what I want for every person who visits All Saints' for the first time. I would like for every visitor who comes through our door to sense that this is a place where the love of Christ abides. That this is a place where, on any given Sunday, each of us can expect an encounter with the Messiah. And maybe more importantly, that we leave this sacred space in anticipation of an encounter with the resurrected Christ in the face of every curious waiter, overbearing teacher, insolent student, demanding patient, tackless physician, insistent client, unreasonable boss, and irritating officemate. The challenge is to realize that in each of these encounters is an opportunity to meet Jesus over and over again.

Church Shopping

As a church planter, I come into contact with quite a few people who tell me they are shopping for a church. Sometimes I feel like I'm standing behind a fast food counter and the church shopper is placing his order, "I'd like a medium-sized church, thinly sliced preaching, go light on the demands, cut the politics, could you make it friendly, and, if you've got 'em, throw in a side of good business contacts." I've been as guilty of church shopping as anyone else. In fact, an innovative church I once "shopped" in California was known by my friends as "The Church of What's Happening Now, Baby."

One Sunday, a delightful young couple visited All Saints'. He was formerly Baptist and she was raised Roman Catholic. They were the kind of couple any church would want to add to their membership roll: clear-eyed, energetic, and planning a family. They seemed to enjoy the worship service and stayed for coffee hour. A number of people stopped by their table to greet them and they clearly felt welcomed. As they were leaving they explained to me that they were new in town, had been visiting a variety of different churches, and were looking for a church that met all of their needs.

It's not the first time I've heard such a statement from "church shoppers." When I ask what sort of "needs" they are talking about I usually get a reply like, "Well, you know, nice music, good preaching, friendly people, Christian education, something for the kids, a pleasant atmosphere." This visiting couple told me of their long-time search for a church that was just right. They would visit one church and find it friendly, but too conservative. At another, they liked the music, but didn't care for the preaching. One was too far from their house. Another didn't have the program they wanted for their future kids. There is nothing wrong with wanting any of those things; it is the kind of thing that everyone would look for in churches. As participants in a culture of consumption, we tend to put the selection of churches in the same category as choosing an automobile, a smart phone, or a piece of luggage.

As consumers, I'd like for people to be happy with their "church experience" on a Sunday morning, but that's not really the business we are in at All Saints'. We're not a hotel chain or an airline; consumer satisfaction is not our objective. We are in the business of transformation. Over the years, I've had a lot of people tell me what they are looking for in a church. One of these days, I dearly desire to hear someone tell me: "I'm looking for a place that will change me." I want somebody to say, "I'm looking for a glimpse of the kingdom of heaven" or "I want a place that will challenge my beliefs and make me uncomfortable with an old way of being." I want somebody to declare that they are tired of the way they are now and that they want to be reacquainted with Jesus and be transformed.

Meeting potential parishioners is a lot like dating. They are sizing me up and I am looking them over. Of course, the process is a little one sided. There are plenty of churches in Bentonville looking for new members. A church accepts, or is supposed to accept, all visitors. But I'll admit that I have my own criteria for what I'm looking for in a parishioner as well. I've imagined what it would be like to have a couple of visitors appear at the church on a Wednesday afternoon, knock quietly on my office door, and say, "Sir, we wish to see Jesus."

If that request happens here, on a Wednesday afternoon while our food pantry is in full swing, I'll probably lead them down the stairs, into the parish hall, where they will find the air filled with the fragrance of sautéed onions and peppers and the sounds of kitchen volunteers slicing and dicing and preparing to feed the hungry. I'd lead this couple who desire to see Jesus to a table where they will meet Bob—jobless, toothless, and, as you would see if he were to remove his worn right shoe, toeless after a bout with diabetes. I would lead them over to Sarah, who is new in town, younger than the lines on her face suggest, who has a husband out looking for work in an old Chevy that doubles as their home and three children who are busily scribbling with a clutch of crayons at the table. Pointing at these folks, I would say to the visitors: "Allow me to introduce you to Jesus." It's really a matter of intention. If we declare our intention to find Jesus in the faces of those we encounter, then we are likely to see him wherever we look.

If I were to try to distill the essence of what it means to live a Christian life, it wouldn't be based on doctrine, belief, or even moral mandate. Instead, I think that the Christian life I aspire to lead is one in which, every morning, when I raise my head from my pillow and open my eyes, I would do so with the expectation and the desire to see Jesus. Whether I raise my eyes to the heavens, walk into a crowded room, or negotiate traffic, the Christian I want to be would make the same request expressed by the Greeks in Jerusalem, "Sir, we wish to see Jesus."

When you begin to encounter the Christ in those around you, you also grow to recognize the Christ within you. The compassion that you learn to show toward others can enable you to show compassion for yourself, to forgive yourself, to accept yourself, and maybe even believe in the higher self you aspire to be. On occasion, a glimpse of Jesus just might even appear in your mirror.

Sowing with Abandon

Since arriving in Bentonville, I've received, at least to my face, nothing but kind words and encouragement from fellow clergy working in the many churches that dot the map of Benton County. But one afternoon, a friend of a friend confided in me that our work here establishing a mission of the Episcopal Church had become a topic of discussion among various pastors. Their conversation went something like this: "I don't know how they can imagine that they can start a church the way they are doing it. Reaching out to all kinds of people, welcoming people who don't belong here to start with, letting in gays and not even trying to change them, going out of their way to welcome blacks and Mexicans. . . and don't they know that if they are going to build a church they are going to need some people of means? People show up there on Sunday dressed every which way. And I can't even tell what they believe. It sure doesn't seem to be the Bible. Letting anybody in? People need unity. They need to know that on Sunday morning they will be sitting beside people like themselves. What kind of a way is that to start a church?"

What kind of way, indeed? Maybe it is the very way that Jesus taught, with his word and by his example. He taught that as planters, we should fling the seed in every direction, allow the seed to fly and fall where it will, and take root in all the most unlikely places. When I first came to town, a few well-meaning folks introduced me to bank officials, chamber of commerce presidents, newspaper editors, and real estate developers. I was received graciously and

I threw seeds in those directions. Some took root, but, by and large, such ground proved to be a little stony. Those who are well established in the community typically have no trouble already being accepted wherever they go. Following the example of the extravagant sower, I held on to the vision that a proper church planter should treat seeds as if they were as bountiful as the love of God. I cast the seeds far and wide without regard for where they landed.

I imagine Jesus's sower, standing in the middle of a field, carrying a large burlap bag of seed draped over a single shoulder with the bag wide-open, so full that the seeds spill over the top and onto the ground. The sower reaches in the bag and scoops up a magnificent handful of seeds and flings them as far as he can in every direction, whirling round and round, pacing in ever expanding circles, covering every surface of the field and his neighbors' field with precious, inexhaustible seed. And no amount of seed taken from the bag diminishes the abundance of seed contained therein. It is the same with the love of God. The more love we offer, the more love we have. The sower of love discovers that God's love knows no limits.

As we begin to understand the nature of the love of God, our own ability to love beyond the boundaries we once knew can also grow. Sowing seed widely serves to expand our circle of compassion. As we scatter seeds about and they sprout and find root, we find ourselves sharing the garden with all of God's created beings. As we encounter people of other colors, cultures, circumstances, and identities, the opportunity to grow compassionate toward them increases. Like the sower in the parable, we are scattering the seeds of love widely. Many seeds fall on stony ground, others are scattered amidst the thorns, and a few are baked by the sun. However, some will sprout, take root, and grow. Before we know it, a garden will spring up, bear fruit, and yield an abundance of love and compassion.

When I first came to Bentonville, I had business cards printed that I would hand out to the folks I met. The cards had a simple message: "The Episcopal Community of Bentonville, Roger Joslin, Church Planter." A year or two later, when the diocese recognized our mission status, the cards read: "All Saints' Episcopal Church."

My title on the card was revised: "Roger Joslin, Vicar and Church Planter." When I ran out of that second set of cards, I considered dropping the "church planter" title. After all, All Saints' was planted. However, I reconsidered after reading the parable of the sower. Instead of keeping the title to myself, I think every member of All Saints' should have business cards that read: "Bill (or Barbara, Chris, Carolyn, or Tim): Church Planter." And just like the sower in the parable, the members can take their cards and scatter them to the four winds, until they rain down like confetti, land on the good earth, take root, and grow.

Fishers of Fish

As I mentioned earlier, my church planting strategy included attending most any event where I could meet people and encounter potential parishioners. A friend invited me to attend a noonday Rotary Club meeting in Bentonville's sister city of Rogers. Stepping into the lobby of the hotel where the group met, my attention immediately fell on a strikingly beautiful woman standing behind the event's registration desk. She welcomed me, introduced herself as Cindee, and apparently noticing my clerical collar, asked if I would be willing to offer a prayer before the meal. Of course, I agreed.

I had often heard the stale prayers offered at these functions and was determined not to follow the pattern of offering thanksgiving to God for all "the benefits so richly deserved by those gathered in this blessed assembly." Instead, I offered a prayer on behalf of the poor, the hungry, and the stranger, but if anyone noticed, they didn't let on. Perhaps Cindee did, since she strolled over after the meeting had ended and thanked me for the prayer. She then asked me how I felt about Israel. Within five minutes it became clear that we disagreed on all things political and religious. We did agree to continue the discussion over coffee. And so began a tumultuous nine-month courtship, culminating in a marriage that was celebrated as part of the Sunday morning Eucharist at St. Thomas

Episcopal Church, in nearby Springdale, Arkansas. I had acquired a partner in the church planting enterprise, and a companion I had never imagined I would meet in Arkansas.

One Monday, Cindee and I took the day off. I awakened that morning with an unusual desire to catch a big fish. I'm not sure where the impulse came from. Perhaps it was born from a legacy passed on from days of fishing with my late father, or maybe it was from this crazy idea I have that if we harvested all the food we needed from our quarter acre of rocky hillside and from the lake that laps at the shore below, our carbon footprint on the earth would be a little smaller. Maybe I was just weary of being only a fisher of people. In a short time, I managed to convince Cindee that we should set out a trotline and catch our supper.

I had seen this process done before, but not since I was a child, when my brothers, my father, and I would pull dozens of catfish from the twisting waters of the Brazos River in Central Texas. We called it the "Bra-zas River," but I later learned that the river had been named by the early Spanish setters "Brazos" after "Los Brazos de Dios," which is translated into English as "The Arms of God." Our Anglicized way of referring to the Brazos River never conveyed just how embraced I felt by that river and those times with my family. Armed with a vision of good times and a plentiful harvest of fish, Cindee and I climbed into our rather tippy canoe, tied one end of the trotline to our dock, and paddled out into the cove to tie the other end of the hook-filled line to the opposite shore.

In almost no time, we were thoroughly entangled in an elaborate mess of fishhooks, twisted string, and stinkbait. A good number of the baited hooks immediately sank into the expectant arms of a submerged maple tree. It only took a couple of tugs on the tangled line, and Cindee reaching out just a tiny bit too far beyond the edge of the canoe, to send me flying out of the boat and into the morass of trotline, tree limbs, and icy water. It was a baptism of sorts.

I sputtered to the surface and climbed into the boat. The apprehensive look on my new wife's face told me that she didn't know how I would react. When I smiled at her, she smiled back in relief and we laughed and laughed. Eventually, we collected ourselves, untangled the trotline, re-baited the dangling hooks, secured the ends of the line, and left the house to attend a Monday night lecture. Returning home well after dark, armed with our flashlight, we made our way down to the dock. I lifted the line, revealing a succession of disappointingly empty hooks, until halfway across the cove I could see, reflecting in the light beam, the wide head and muscled upper body of a ten-pound catfish. Within the hour, I cleaned the fish, bathed it in olive oil, garlic, and spices and placed it in a hot oven. We steamed some kale. And then, in a fitting celebration, Cindee suggested that we have martinis. And so we dined, like some royal Arkansas hillbillies, on martinis, catfish, and kale.

Authentic Mission

Arriving from the west, not by boat but rather by pickup truck (I must have had some precognition that while the skills of preaching, teaching, and pastoral care might be useful for a church planter, it was absolutely essential that one own a pickup truck), I began the task of observing the foreign culture in which I had landed. I first noticed that the natives drank a sugary beverage called sweet tea, so sweet that it actually made my teeth hurt. And it wasn't long before I realized that when I heard one of the natives say, "Well, bless your heart," I hadn't necessarily found a convert.

After careful observation, I came to the conclusion that the primitive belief system of the native Arkansawyers revolved around the exultation and adoration of swine; they were pig worshipers. My initial hint that this might be the case happened at my first visit to a barbeque joint, where I noticed that, before the sacred pork was consumed, it was ritually pulled apart, by what I took to be the priestly class standing before stainless steel altars, wearing grease-stained white vestments hidden from view in steamy kitchens.

And then in the fall, which I took to be the holiest of seasons, with Saturdays apparently the highest holy day, most of the natives were festooned in fiery red costumes, as if it were the day of Pentecost. Emblazoned on the front of their garments was the image of their deity, the ubiquitous and legendary razorback hog. On Saturday afternoons, the natives would gather around their televisions (or those who could would make the pilgrimage to the Mecca of Fayetteville) and watch as young men, selected for their athletic prowess, engaged in a highly ritualized combat with neighboring tribes over the possession of the sacred pigskin. And then, occasionally, as the battle between the young warriors heightened, the voices of the worshipers, as if collectively possessed by a primitive impulse to cry out in praise of their deity, would simultaneously emit a fierce, high pitched, chant: "Wooooooooooo, Pig! Sooie!"

My guess is that the Apostle Paul, having crossed the Aegean Sea on his first missionary journey from Asia to Europe, must have experienced a similar culture shock. Paul had intended to sail to the Bithynia in northern Asia Minor, but he was led by a vision to change his course and, instead, go to the Roman colony of Philippi. The trip could have turned out very differently. Twice, scripture tells that the Holy Spirit redirected Paul away from Asia toward Europe. The erratic winds blowing Paul's vessel across the Aegean Sea could have carried him to a coastal city other than Philippi. Even still, he could have, by chance, arrived on a Sunday and missed the Sabbath prayers held outside the gate by the river, where Lydia had joined her Jewish neighbors to pray.

Lydia, herself, could have missed the prayers that day; she could have been detained by one of the Roman officers who retired in Philippi, who, unrespecting of the Sabbath, took his time in selecting just the right purple fabric for his new robe from among the many bolts of purple cloth Lydia sold in the market. Or perhaps Lydia, a Greek Gentile, might never have even been drawn to Judaism at all, were it not for a Jewish neighbor or customer in whom she had observed a quiet devotion, a spirit-filled existence, or a sense of community that she desired for herself. If Lydia hadn't attended the prayers that day, she wouldn't have encountered Paul. Lydia would not have become the first European Christian convert and Paul's mission to Europe could possibly have ground to a screeching halt, were it not for Lydia's insistence that her home provide him sanctuary. The faith and generosity of Lydia, a dealer in purple cloth, just might have altered history.

It often seems miraculous that I wound up here in Bentonville, planting the progressive church of All Saints'. There were so many obstacles in the way. Yet each time an obstacle appeared, so did a new pathway. A wise priest would offer good counsel or a word on my behalf. A chance encounter would open a door. All the while, the town of Bentonville was growing and changing in ways that made the establishment of a vibrant Episcopal church a possibility. The prospect of a mission here was greatly aided by an Arkansas woman who, after a lifetime of faithful membership in her small parish, decided that a portion of her estate would be used to fund the development of new congregations. So much seemed to occur by chance, and so much by an earnest desire on the part of God's faithful people to follow God's will.

I'm not among those who readily accept tired clichés. When I hear someone say that "God has a plan," I tend to flinch and think that if that's true, then the plan seems pretty messed up for a whole lot of people. I'm more inclined to think that we are called to seek purpose in whatever circumstances we find ourselves. We are all missionaries; we all have a mission and we all have a purpose. Opportunities for missionary work abound at All Saints', in music, worship, hospitality, pastoral care, feeding the hungry, and caring for the imprisoned. Maybe, like Lydia, a successful dealer in purple cloth, a person is even in a position to substantially support the mission of the church by sharing what they have. Richard Landers has written, "Authentic mission is always a response to need within the community, not simply the missionary's need to proclaim." It seems to me that arriving at "authentic mission" is the result of a miraculous convergence of steadfast faithfulness and divine direction. Just as he called the Apostle Paul, God has called each of us to proclaim good news, in whatever way we can. Welcome to the missionary journey.

CHAPTER 3

The Mission Appears

Declare his glory among the nations, his marvelous works among all the peoples.

—1 Chronicles 16:24

Jesus said, "The kingdom of God is as if someone would scatter seed on the ground, and would sleep and rise night and day, and the seed would sprout and grow" (Mark 4:26–27). As one who plans on raising a few vegetables on the rocky hillsides in the unforgiving soil of Northwest Arkansas, I'm struck by the easy, casual way the farmer in Jesus's parable goes about planting his fields. There is no mention of tilling the soil in preparation for the seeds, irrigating, or doing battle with weeds, insects, or the diseases that run amok in my garden. The farmer simply scatters his seeds aimlessly and shows up later to enjoy the harvest. It's a far cry from the hardscrabble life of the original Ozark hill people who, without the dietary supplement provided by whatever critters they could blast out of the trees or the profits generated from the sale of moon-shine, would likely have starved to death their first winter.

It is probably helpful to remember that Jesus was the son of a carpenter and not a farmer. But more than finding employment as a carpenter or as a farmer, Jesus was a sower of the seeds of the word of God. And what he could see around him was that the seeds of the word were already quickly taking root. Those seeds had landed on the ground and were sprouting and growing in a way that must have surprised him. The time and place for Jesus's message was right. There was unease in the land. The character of the Jewish faith was shifting. The Roman occupation brought prosperity and poverty; both existed side by side. Opportunity and fear were prevalent among the people. While prophets and miracle workers of every sort rose up in the land, it was Jesus's message of love, redemption, and salvation that remained with the people. It was a message that found a patch of moist, life-sustaining ground and began to flourish.

The parables we find in Mark's Gospel were recorded decades after Jesus told the stories, even after the Apostle Paul had taken Jesus's message to the Gentiles and had spread the good news to the far reaches of the Roman Empire. The compiler of Mark's Gospel, with his own historical perspective, would have understood just how fertile the ground for Jesus's message had been in a way that Jesus himself could never have imagined. Indeed, the time was right at that moment for the faith of a small Jewish sect, infused with the love of Christ, to find roots and be transformed into a major world religion.

Bentonville is located on fertile land, in the sense that the ground on which we live and work in Northwest Arkansas is, at this particular moment in time, rich, moist, and ready for seeds of change to sprout and flourish. We live in a time and place where change can happen, a land where a few seeds scattered can take root, a place where a Walmart employee or a Walmart vendor can make a real difference in the way the world looks. The presence of vibrant international commerce has resulted in a population that is as ethnically and geographically diverse as any small town in America. It's a land where great wealth beyond that ever imagined by the Roman emperors exists side by side with great poverty. It's an area where people with skin tones of every shade who come to engage in trade can find both a warm welcome and suffer harsh discrimination. It's a place of an unspoken clash between the values of raw capitalism and a Christian desire for humility, self-giving, and compassion.

There exists here the potential to remold the message of Christianity in a way that is more in keeping with the original message of Christ's love and compassion. Change has come so rapidly over the past decade to this little corner of the Ozarks that people have come to expect change. And that has presented members of a progressive church plant such as All Saints' with the incredible opportunity to become agents for change in a place where everyone can truly make a difference.

Smokin' Out Gophers

"Supposing him to be the gardener, she said to Jesus, 'Sir, if you have carried him away, tell me where you have laid him, and I will take him away'" (John 20:15). Mary Magdalene wasn't the first, nor was she the last, to misunderstand the gardener's true identity. It was early spring and I had only arrived in Bentonville just a few weeks prior. One evening, I was taking a walk through the neighborhood surrounding my garage apartment when I stumbled upon a beautiful garden. No signage indicated whether it was a public or private garden and there was no gate barring the entrance. Since it had an inviting quality, I decided to wander in. The garden was in full bloom. Azaleas, dogwoods, redbuds, and a great variety of other flowers filled the carefully tended beds and lined the path passing through the garden. I sat on a bench and considered my good fortune at discovering such a delightful oasis so close to my home. Then, out of the corner of my eye, I noticed a small cloud of smoke rising from the ground. Kneeling on the ground beside the smoke was an old man who was clad in the all-khaki shirt and pants, which, for men of an earlier generation, meant that there was work to be done.

I sat on the bench and enjoyed the birds and the flowers. Eventually, out of some concern for the still-kneeling figure in the garden's corner but probably more out of curiosity, I wandered down the path in the direction of the old man. I considered the possibility that he might be praying, yet as I grew closer, I could see that, although he was in a posture of prayer, his eyes were open and fixed on the mound of dirt in front of him. Fearing that I might startle him, I shuffled a bit and cleared my throat. "Evening," I offered.

"Evening," he replied.

"Everything, okay?" I asked.

"Fine," he answered, adjusting his position. He had clearly been on his knees too long. Scattered around him were several torn cellophane wrappers, matches, and a couple of torpedo shaped objects with fuses at one end that resembled stubby firecrackers.

"If you don't mind my asking, what are you doing?" I inquired.

"Ahh," he said, "just smokin' out gophers."

I was in college in the sixties, and smoking gophers sounded rather reminiscent of a common recreational activity of that era. I didn't expect to find that it was a practice of the elderly here in Arkansas.

But it was the furry underground rodents that this gardener was after and he fervently desired to rid them from his flowerbeds. Apparently, he had never witnessed the frustration of Bill Murray in the film *Caddyshack* or he would have let the gophers be. As he lit fuses, buried the smoke bombs, and patiently watched the tiny wisps of smoke rise from fissures in the soil, the gardener began to talk. He told me of the garden, how it had once been filled with trash and how he and his sons had hauled off old cars and abandoned refrigerators. He showed me how some of the azaleas, in an area where rust and chemicals once resided, still failed to prosper. As he talked of his garden, bits of his larger story began to unfold.

Nestled within his descriptions of exotic plants, I caught hints of his travels to equally exotic lands. Contained within his conversation about plant selection and land reclamation, his business acumen was revealed. Sprinkled in his stories about family and friends, I caught a glimpse of how connected this khaki-clad old gardener really was. It wasn't long before I was able to ascertain that the old man I had encountered on his knees smoking out gophers wasn't merely a gardener but, because of his long association with Sam Walton, probably one of the wealthiest men I had ever met.

This garden we call All Saints' is a place of resurrection. It is the kind of place where Mary Magdalene can hear the Christ call her by name and she can recognize his voice. It is the kind of place where we might learn that the humble gardener is the Christ himself.

Laundromat Stories

A laundromat in Arkansas can be a rather grim place, but that is where I would find myself every other Sunday evening upon my initial arrival in Bentonville. If I'm at the grocery store, the coffee shop, or the business supply place, I use the opportunity to meet people and look for prospective parishioners. On my first visit to the laundromat, I met a really nice young man whose family had emigrated to the U.S. from Thailand. I readily told him about our plans for a church and gave him my business card.

The second visit to the laundromat was different. When I walked into the overly bright laudromat, I was overtaken by enough cigarette smoke to make me think I was in a West Texas bar. A scantily clad young woman had draped her ample posterior over three plastic chairs. The first thing I noticed was the vast expanse of painfully red skin displayed between the straps of her loose-fitting sundress. She must have weighed over 350 pounds. Six blond kids raced around her, past me, and toward their father. All were sunburned badly. The father was thin, the kind of thin that comes when a man prefers smoking cigarettes to eating. Both of them sucked on Camels, burning them to the filters. They both yelled at the kids to settle down.

One of the children walked up and stared at me. "Have you been to the river?" I asked.

"I caught a perch," he replied.

Suddenly, I was surrounded by five other dirty, sunburned, towheaded, barefoot kids, each telling me how they had or hadn't caught a perch and that daddy had caught a catfish "this big," indicating the size of the fish by separating their small hands at a distance. "Daddy" was leaning up against a row of rusty washing machines and, taking one deep drag after another, watched me warily. A toddler wearing a sagging diaper, in his best imitation of his big brothers, made his way to a place a few inches in front of me and simply looked up at me and grinned. From his outstretched orange-stained fingers, he offered me one of his Cheetos.

I chatted with the woman about their float-trip adventures tubing down the river and about how they had so much fun that they were going again the following Thursday. I'm usually pretty quick about handing out my business card; I take this church-planting thing rather seriously and I'll talk to anyone because I want to plant an inclusive church. I want the church that I plant to practice a kind of radical hospitality, the same kind that Jesus was known for and was ultimately executed for. I make a lot of noise about this being the kind of church where all are welcome.

That evening, I told my son Nate about my experience at the laundromat. He listened intently, as he usually does to my many stories. He appreciated the image I painted of the barefoot kids and enormous expanse of sunburned skin. But when I finished telling the tale, he asked a question that brought the story to an abrupt end: "Dad, did you give them your card?"

I would have liked to have told my son that I did. I wished that I had told the family that we were planting a church and that they would be welcome there, but I didn't. Sometimes, I find myself looking for a more desirable class of poor people to welcome to the church at the cost of unintentionally excluding others. I had left after putting my clothes in one of the washing machines and driven back to my home.

Now, feeling guilty, I went back to the laundromat hoping to see them still there, but when I arrived they had already loaded their clothes and kids into their rusted out Dodge Caravan and left for home.

Later, while folding my clothes, I struck up a conversation with another woman and her two boys. Like the other family, the two kids, Jacob and Charles, chased each other through the labyrinth of washers and dryers. This mom wouldn't have allowed her kids to get so badly sunburned and when the younger boy hit his head, she held him tightly and made him laugh. I told her of our church plans and gave her my card, proving to myself that it is indeed easier to welcome a better class of poor people to the church.

The following Friday evening included yet another "missionary journey" to the laundromat. I met a woman who, upon learning that I was a priest, smiled broadly and said, "I've never met a priest before." I felt sort of like a rare bird being viewed by an ornithologist, but she meant well. Within five minutes, I had learned that her husband was in jail and expected to serve a sentence of five to ten years.

"I'm sorry, that must be hard," I said, in my best pastor's voice.

"I'm not. I'm glad. Last night, he tried to strangle me," she said, pulling the collar down on her blouse to show me the red streaks on her neck.

I looked at her beautiful daughter. Her light brown skin and slightly Asian features foretold a time when she would capture the attention of any man not held prisoner by Arkansan prejudice. Her name was Asia and she watched and listened as her mother told stories of her angry father. My mind raced forward to a time when this woman, or another equally poor and equally open woman, would be in my parish and occupy the attention and prayers of the people. The difficult twists of her life were laid out for me to see, not just because the poor like to talk about their problems, but because they can't afford the well constructed houses that are surrounded by vast expanses of lawns and gated communities that hide their troubles from society. Their lives are splayed open and their suffering is evident to all who don't turn their head; they can't afford the rich man's luxury of private pain.

I gave her my card and told her to call me if I could help. I've learned from these frequent visits to the laundromat that class can be a far more formidable barrier to full acceptance in a church than race or even sexual orientation.

It Is Good for Us to Be Here

I cannot be sure about my own face, but on the Sunday morning when the people that had been meeting in small groups for six or eight months first gathered together to celebrate the Eucharist, their faces were glowing. They had waited for this day for some time. For decades, generations before them had dreamed of the day when there would be an Episcopal Church in Bentonville. Those whom I had gotten to know through meeting in our various small groups and those who shared their stories with me in coffee shops and cafés were, at last, worshiping together in a school auditorium. It looked a lot like church. Like Moses on the mountaintop, their faces are glowing, perhaps even transfigured. Like Peter, I was tempted to say, "It is good for us to be here; let's make three dwellings—one for Moses, one for Elijah, one for Jesus—and let's settle in."

When I was a kid, I loved to build dwellings. I would drape my mother's sheets and blankets across an assemblage of chairs and tables, creating tent-like hiding places in the living room. Later, every scrap heap became a source of building material for the forts and tree houses that eventually dotted the valley below my family's small ranch, most with a sign clearly posted on the outside that read: "Girls Keep Out!" Later, a dense bamboo forest along the creek bed became the haven for an entire village of bamboo huts that were populated by my savage, marauding band of eleven-year-old friends.

But the dwelling that was our crowning glory was created from a haystack. By midsummer, our barn was filled to the rafters with bales of sweet-smelling Coastal Bermuda hay, which was the result of two abundant harvests and much labor spent hauling the hay from the fields on flatbed trailers and systematically stacking row upon row into the barn. All this work was done so that the cows would have plenty of fodder to feed them through the winter.

However, as the long Texas summer wore on, we eventually grew bored with our bamboo huts and tree houses. Our gang turned its collective attention to the haystack and we began to rearrange the bales. Working harder than we had ever worked in the fields, we created a series a tunnels and rooms within the hay, a labyrinthine network replete with trap doors, false turns, dead ends, and, for those willing to crawl on their bellies through the itchy hay and endless darkness, a sanctuary that was hidden deep within the heart of the haystack. This inner room was large enough for us to stand up or sprawl about, but mostly, we sat cross-legged in a circle, our dimming flashlights placed upright in the middle of the ring pointed skyward. We shared our childhood secrets and talked of our dreams of what we would become and thought: "It is good for us to be here." And it was. That is, until the winter came.

One cold, January evening, I remember my Dad coming into the house after he had been feeding the cows. It was usually my job, but I had gone to a basketball game that night and he had taken over my chores. Dad said, "Son, did you know that our haystack is hollow? I thought we had more feed for the cattle. There isn't enough hay to get the cows through the winter."

In our ecstasy of creating a satisfying dwelling, in our eagerness to proclaim that "It is good for us to be here," we had created an empty shell. Rather than being filled with the sustenance that the cattle needed to sustain them through the winter, our haystack was simply a cavernous void; it was an illusion of abundance, concealing an empty crater hidden deep within.

Upon learning that I am a church planter, one of the first questions that people typically ask me is: "When are you going to build a church?"

I patiently respond by saying, "Well, you know, the church really isn't about the building. It's about the people. We are building a community; we think that God is in the relationship, so we are focused on creating and sustaining sacred relationships."

People usually respond by smiling and nodding in agreement saying, "Yeah, yeah, that's right. . . but where do you think you will put the church?"

Abraham Joshua Heschel wrote a book with a simple title, *The Sabbath*. In the book, Heschel writes of how technical civilization is largely about the conquest of space. He says that technical civilization is the result of man's desire to "subdue and manage the forces of nature—things, tools, houses, manufacturing, special surroundings." He points out how this same spatial orientation extends into the world of religion. We think of a God that resides in particular places, mountains, forests, temples, cathedrals, shrines, and sacred spaces. But as Heschel notes, "a god who can be fashioned, a god who can be confined, is but a shadow of man." Instead, consider the notion that we find God much less in the creation of scared spaces, than we find God in the recognition of holy moments and sacred relationships. We live in a world where the measure of a church is taken by its magnificence and the prominence of its building. Time itself is sacred as well.

I do not intend to overlook the importance of sacred space. Indeed, on the Sunday before our first Eucharist, when we gathered to unload and arrange the altar, the pulpit, the lectern, the baptismal font, and even the bishop's chair, I was amazed at the transformation of the space. A junior high auditorium, which was filled the day before with noisy, smelly, prepubescent kids, was transformed into a place where we were inclined to speak in hushed tones. Even the furniture glowed, though that might have just been from the lemon oil.

What we shared on that first Sunday was, by any measure, one of those mountaintop experiences. The introduction of a few pieces of furniture and the presence of a few hopeful would-be parishioners transformed an ordinary junior high auditorium into a place that felt a lot like church. For the very first time, we broke bread together as a community and experienced the shared body and blood of Christ. It was historic. And, indeed, it was good for us to be there. It was good to relish the moment, as it had been a long time in the making. However, if we had allowed ourselves to think that we had now become the church we had long hoped for, we would have remained as hollow as the tunnel-riddled haystack of my childhood.

I used to be asked, usually when I said something slightly heretical and before I began to wear my collar, a peculiar question: "Are you a Christian?"

My favorite reply was usually: "No, but I would really like to be." I think of myself more as a "Jesus follower," as one who aspires to be a Christian. And although what had looked and felt like a church that day was real, I believed that we should stay in the process of becoming a church for as long as we could.

At our first Eucharist, we were still an emerging church. The church that we were going to look like six months into the future was a little difficult for us to fully comprehend. Those who were gathered in the auditorium came from a variety of backgrounds. A few were Episcopalian, but many were Baptists, Methodists, Roman Catholics, those who had claimed no denomination, others who had no church affiliation, and even some who questioned God's existence. While our expectations of what church should be about varied widely, we were all God's children; each one of us loved by the Divine One. And every one who had gathered felt welcome.

While we celebrate our diversity, I think that a common thread that binds us is a shared belief, or at least a common hope, that God can be found in community. I've heard the bishop of the Diocese of Atlanta say that God is not simply in relationship, but that God is relationship. In the formation of this emerging church, we have relied heavily on the "small group model." Relational groups are at the core of this congregation. These groups are our heart and soul. As beautiful as it is to gather here on a Sunday morning, if we are truly to be in close relationship with one another, we need a chance to hear each other's stories, to know one another deeply. Without that intimate knowledge of one another, our chances of becoming a real church, a church that is more than walls, steeples, and giant crosses, are really slim to none.

In our "Theology Pub," a small group that meets regularly in which members can explore questions not commonly asked in church, we probed a way of thinking of how God acts in the world called process theology. Process theology is all about relationship. In that relationship, God changes us and we, in turn, change God. All of creation is linked together in this web of being and sharing love. A principle tenet of process theology is that God isn't an omnipotent being that sits apart from the world and directs events here on earth, causing earthquakes and hurricanes or intervening directly in the minutia of existence. Rather, a process theologian would say that we worship a God without hands. In other words, God acts in the world through each of us and we are called to be the hands of God.

We are called into relationship with God, not merely to bask in the glory of a mountaintop experience, but to experience the love of God in relationship with one another. It is in and through relationship and by experiencing the diversity that is God's creation that we learn to live into the challenge of being the vehicle through which God acts in the world, thereby accepting what it means to be the hands of God. As the Franciscan priest Richard Rohr has said, "We need relationships of duration and truth to unveil our faces so that we can reflect like mirrors the brightness of the Lord." My prayer is that as a still emerging Christian community, we will "all grow brighter and brighter as we are gradually turned into the image that we reflect; this is the work of the Lord who is Spirit" (2 Cor. 3:18).

CHAPTER 4

The Mission Unfolds

And he said to them, "Go into all the world and proclaim the good news to the whole creation."

—Mark 16:15

Methodist and Baptist circuit rider priests in the "Old West" started churches throughout the United States. Episcopalians waited until there was a courthouse, a nice hotel, and a decent restaurant before planting their own. In Northwest Arkansas, the Episcopal Church did much the same thing. Long after every other denomination had multiple churches in Bentonville, there was still no Episcopal Church. The politically conservative and religiously fundamentalist climate in the city made it seem like an unlikely place to successfully plant a broad-minded outpost.

When I hear the story about the decision of the fishermen from Galilee to hang around long enough to find out what was going on with the carpenter from Nazareth, I can't help but think of the people of All Saints' and their willingness to join together to create this church. I'm aware that a few years ago more than one resident expressed their skepticism concerning this Texan's early efforts to form an Episcopal community in Bentonville. There were questions along the same lines of Nathanael's inquiry, "Can anything good come out of Nazareth?" (John 1:46). Before my arrival it may have been asked, "Can anything good come out of Texas?" This reminds me of the populist commentator, Molly Ivins, who once scolded her fellow Texans, "Next time I tell you someone from Texas should not be president of the United States, please pay attention." But despite my roots in the Lone Star State, many in Northwest Arkansas were kind and patient with me and have enthusiastically joined together to form this community of Jesus followers.

I like how John's Gospel depicts the way that Jesus started his missionary journey, "The next day, Jesus decided to go to Galilee" (John 1:43). The decision to go to Galilee isn't presented as a grand epiphany; there is no angelic summons. Instead, you get the impression that Jesus might have been simply eating his Post Toasties cereal and drinking his second cup of coffee, while suddenly saying to himself: "I think I'll go to Galilee today." Maybe in much the same way that many of our parishioners one Sunday morning decided to come to All Saints'. However, not everyone is as easily convinced to visit a progressive church plant like All Saints' for the first time.

I'm rather drawn to the honest skepticism of Nathanael about what he had heard from his brother about Jesus. Christians, if they can be honest with themselves, are pretty skeptical about what passes for Christianity among the true believers. Phillip didn't try to convince his friend Nathanael that he had to believe anything. Instead, he simply suggested that Nathanael "come and see."

And when Nathanael "came to see," he found that Jesus knew more about him than he could have ever imagined. Nathanael regarded Jesus's insight, his knowledge that Nathanael sat under the fig tree before Phillip called him, as something of a miracle. The initial miracle, I suggest, was that Jesus was beginning to open Nathanael's eyes to the miracles that were soon to come.

And there, in Galilee, Jesus began to collect his disciples: Simon Peter and his brother Andrew, their friend Phillip, and Nathanael, who witnessed the small miracle and believed. John's Gospel indicates that it was after this fateful encounter in Galilee that Jesus and this new collection of disciples went to the wedding at Cana, where Jesus turned the water into wine. Shortly thereafter, they all went to Jerusalem where Jesus cleansed the temple, met with Nicodemus by night, and began his ministry of preaching, teaching, and healing throughout all of Judea.

The work of progressive church planting is not unlike the work of the early disciples. Like the early disciples, we too have also witnessed a few miracles of our own. During Holy Communion one Sunday in the spring, I witnessed a seemingly endless stream of babies, all held in their parents' arms and ready to receive my blessing. It seemed miraculous to see so many expectant faces. And surrounding these children were other All Saints' parishioners, some who had not attended church for thirty years because they had been wronged by the church, or had never found a church that would accept them. And in their midst were people who, like Nathanael, brought their questions, their intellect, and their skepticism to the altar. They all came forward, one hand placed atop another, ready to receive Christ's body and blood. If that moment was not miraculous enough, I find myself still amazed that right here in Bentonville we have established a thriving Hispanic ministry, the first in the history of the Diocese of Arkansas!

John's Gospel tells us that Nathanael is "an Israelite in whom there is no deceit" (John 1:47). Or, as it says in the King James Version, "no guile." Nathanael is a good, honest, and decent human being. He wasn't the wretched sinner that Bible-thumping preachers like to talk about Jesus coming to save. He was simply a decent person and Jesus chose to make him a disciple. Jesus gave him a purpose, a mission, and a reason for being. For people like us who are seeking a purpose, that alone is a miracle.

What I want to offer is the same assurance that Jesus offered Nathanael: "You will see greater things than these" (John 1:50). Simply by their presence in the early days, the people of All Saints' responded to a call to mission. Each of those who responded to the call are missioners. Some were among the first to be called, like Peter, Andrew, Phillip, and Nathanael. While others, like Matthew, Mark, and Luke were called a little later. Nevertheless, all of us are missioners and each of us has been called, as a follower of Jesus, to bear witness to the miraculous in our midst.

Word came to me that the monthly rent on the "little theater" at the Junior High where we had been meeting on Sunday mornings was going to climb considerably. So it was that I responded joyfully to an invitation from Jeanne, the pastor at Christ the King Lutheran Church in Bentonville, to share their worship space. After months of meeting in a space where the backdrop to the celebration of the Eucharist was likely to be stage set for *Alice in Wonderland* or *The Music Man*, it was with great pleasure that we began worshiping in a space where faithful people of God had gathered to pray for decades. Their prayers seemed to have permeated the brick walls of the nave.

Still, missioners are not typically called to service in the most ideal conditions. None were drawn to All Saints' because of the architectural splendor of our rented space. None came because of the magnificence of our hundred-voice choir, or because they expected to hear Bach played on an organ with twenty thousand pipes and seven manuals, or even because our acolytes move through their paces with flawless precision and military bearing. And no one came here because a life shared with the Lutherans was sweet harmony. Finding convenient parking on Sundays has been near impossible. In order to attend Sunday school classes, we had to climb steep stairs to get to a crowded classroom that doubles as a quilting place. Our vestry often had to meet in the kitchen. We were never quite sure when the Lutherans' service would end so our choir could hurriedly rehearse and the altar guild could set up for our own worship service. The clutter in the parish hall seemed to grow exponentially. And every Advent, a pagan-inspired Christmas tree appeared on the chancel. For us Episcopalians, that's heresy!

But Jesus never told his disciples that following him would be easy. I can only imagine that the early disciples put up with more than a few discomforts. They walked dusty roads, faced ridicule and persecution, and depended on the kindness of strangers for their sustenance. All of this discomfort was endured for an opportunity to experience a daily encounter with the Divine. Jesus's call of Phillip and Nathanael was not only a call to mission; it was a call to recognize the presence of God in their daily lives.

This story stands at the crossroads of discipleship and Christology. In our walk with Jesus, we learn who he is and who we are as well. We learn what we are made of. Are we seeking comfort or are we seeking challenge? Do we seek to surround ourselves with those things that serve us or are we called to a life of servanthood ourselves? Jesus promised to Nathanael that if he would walk with him he would see "heaven opened and the angels of God ascending and descending upon the Son of Man" (John 1:51). May we too listen for God's voice amidst the miracles and the mundane, the triumphant and the troublesome. May we awaken to the Divine Presence in all we encounter.

No One Wearing Shoes

There is a classic story about two shoe salesmen in the early days of the twentieth century who were commissioned by the owner of the shoe factory to go to Africa and sell shoes. The first shoe salesman telegraphed this message back to the headquarters: "Situation hopeless, no one wears shoes."

The second salesman, however, sent home a different telegram: "Potential unlimited, no one wearing shoes."

When I came to Bentonville to plant a church, I felt a little like these shoe salesmen. After a couple weeks, I could have e-mailed the bishop: "We can't start an Episcopal church here, there aren't any

Episcopalians." Instead, my early messages were something similar to this: "This is a great place to start a church, there aren't any Episcopalians." And Bentonville has proven to be an ideal place to start a church, not only because there aren't any Episcopalians, but also because there is an abundance of people here who hunger and thirst to know God. There are people who are looking for a different way of being Christian. There are people who long to be accepted just as God created them. There are people who don't want to leave their intellect behind when they walk inside a church. There are people who regard the Bible as too rich and powerful merely to be taken literally. There are people who seek an experience of transcendence in worship.

The parishioners of All Saints' have received an astounding gift as well. Most people in Benton County considered progressive and Christian to be a contradiction. However, with God's help, we have created a place where the progressive Christian can now find a home. In the early years, we had a series of gatherings at my house called "cottage meetings." We try to create an atmosphere in which people can share their stories with one another and talk about what brought them to All Saints'. Over and over again, I've heard people talk about reading an article in the local paper. The headline reads: "Progressive church to shake up Benton County scene." I didn't pick the title, but it's funny. I didn't really know that it was our mission to create a progressive church. I simply knew that we were called to create a church in which the love of Christ is offered to everyone, without exception. If that is progressive, then count me in.

Talents

We don't want to miss any opportunity that is presented to us. It is easy enough, when things are tripping along nicely, for us to be caught up in the flow. An economic slowdown gives us a moment to breathe, take a look around, and figure out what it is that is really important to us. And if this business of recognizing the Christ that is in everyone who surrounds us is really important, then we won't be burying our talents, our bags of gold, in the ground. Our opportunity to be of service to the Bentonville community is more real than ever. Our mission to those who are rejected by the larger society is made more vivid in times of economic decline. Rather than retreating, we are called to move forward. In times of economic downturn and uncertainty, times like we are experiencing now, there is a tendency, in any society, to look for scapegoats or people to blame for our troubles and difficulties. During those times, the "other," those who are on the margins of society or those who are simply different, become particularly vulnerable.

All Saints' is already known to be a place that reaches out to those on the margins of society. From its beginnings, it has been a church where neither rigid adherence to a particular set of beliefs, skin color, sexual orientation, gender identity and expression, nor economic class presents a barrier for full participation in our fellowship. All Saints' is a place where people who don't quite fit in elsewhere can find a home. These are the people who, in these difficult times, desperately need a home. We provide a place that recognizes and illustrates every Sunday that a gay parent can be a good parent. Every Sunday, All Saints' is a place that provides us with evidence that the immigrant, whose documents are not in order, still merits our respect and Christian love. It is the kind of place where, on Wednesday evening, you can share a very good meal with someone who, were it not for All Saints', might not eat that evening at all.

As a church, we could decide to retreat. We could decide that having a youth director isn't so important. We could decide that training Godly Play teachers so that our youngest Saints can grasp the nature of God's love is something we can't afford. We could decide that raising our children in an environment of love and acceptance isn't such a big deal after all. We could decide that fostering a music program that uplifts our spirits and puts us in touch with the transcendent is too expensive. And we could decide that the poor don't need to be fed and the outcasts don't need to be welcomed. We could take our single talent, dig a hole in the ground, and hide our master's money.

But the good news that we have to proclaim, the news that the kingdom of heaven is now upon us and that all are welcome to share in the riches of that kingdom, is just too good to keep to ourselves. We could decide that we are too small, too new, and too fragile to take on this great task. But, if we don't do this work, who will? The real gift we have been given is Christ himself. And inherent in that gift is the ability to be Christ for the other and to see Christ in the other. Indeed, living into that gift is the very mission of a church like All Saints'.

Creating Church

On our first celebration of the Day of Pentecost, All Saints' was still meeting in Washington Junior High School's auditorium. Since we had just started holding Sunday morning worship, we were still scrambling around before the service to set up the altar furniture on the stage of the musty theater. In those days, visitors often found themselves recruited to read the lessons, lead the prayers, or sing in the choir as soon as they walked through the door. More than one twelve-year-old boy or girl learned what an acolyte was and had his or her first experience carrying the processional cross on the same day. These were chaotic times, but they provided fertile ground for the Holy Spirit to scatter her seeds.

In just a few months' time, we not only had people prepared to serve as regular readers and acolytes for our church services, but we also had Sunday school teachers, singers for our growing choir, and community organizers eager to evangelize and serve the poor. And it wasn't much longer before we had people who desired to share the Eucharist with the homebound and homeless, gardeners who wanted to start a community garden, and folks who wanted to build clinics. All of our parishioners were yearning to respond to the needs of troubled youth, the unwelcome immigrant, the neglected prisoner, and the friendless in the community.

Our pews are filled with people who have identified needs in the community and who are passionate about bringing their gifts of the Holy Spirit to bear. It is been my great joy to talk with new members of our parish and learn about the gifts and talents they bring with them, continuing a legacy that, while still in its infancy, has become central to who we are as a people. We are a people intent on resurrection, on discovering our passion, and living into it with all of our being.

The Miracle of "Seeing Again"

In Mark's Gospel, blind Bartimaeus cries out to Jesus, "Son of David, have mercy on me!" (Mark 10:48). Elsewhere, the translation reads, "Have pity on me." However, as it was recorded in its original Greek source, Bartimaeus's request, *eleeson me*, wasn't one in which he was asking Jesus to simply look kindly upon him. Bartimaeus's plea is really a call for action. There is no exact English translation for Bartimaeus crying out that Jesus do something about his condition of blindness. If it were an actual word, "mercify me" would be a close approximation of the blind man's desperate desire. "Mercify me," "Let me see again," "Restore my faith" were Bartimaeus's pleas. Again and again, these are the pleas that I have heard since coming to Bentonville. Living in an environment where Christianity is often characterized by ignorance, control, bigotry, and exclusion, I listen to the voices cry out: "Show me how I can once again be a follower of Jesus!" Their "seeing again" is truly a miracle for me to watch unfold.

But the miracle of "seeing again" has happened to me as well. Every Sunday at All Saints', we have a large number of children who receive communion with their parents. One Sunday, we had more children in attendance than usual. I should have expected it, because while we were singing the Sanctus and I was saying the Eucharistic Prayer, joyful baby voices were accompanying our own prayers. To paraphrase the psalmist, "Their mouths were filled with laughter, and their tongues with shouts of joy."

At first, during Holy Communion, nothing seemed out of the ordinary. A few little ones reached out their hands to receive a wafer. They were followed by their mothers and fathers who held their precious infants in their arms, offering their children to me in order to receive a blessing. But then, more children approached the altar. In fact, so many children came up to receive communion that I found myself moved to tears by their outstretched hands and expectant faces. Offering communion every Sunday is one of the greatest privileges of being a priest and I always relish it. But on that particular Sunday, the waves of children that kept coming forward allowed me, like blind Bartimaeus, to "see again." Quite literally, I was seeing the future of our community in these children and infants, a vision of what All Saints' is becoming.

Before coming to Northwest Arkansas, I didn't fully understand the nature of our mission here. I didn't know that by planting an Episcopal Church in the shadow of an empire, the true nature of our endeavor would be to "mercify," to let people "see again," to allow them to discover that their intellect, their belief in science, their sexual orientation, their gender identity and expression, or their love for beauty in worship are not obstacles to an ultimate acceptance of Jesus Christ. I didn't know that we could enable people to "see again" by insisting that the Bible is too precious, too important, to be taken literally. And I didn't know that by accepting the legitimacy and the sanctity of the path to God chosen by our Buddhist, Jewish, Hindu, and Muslim brothers and sisters we would enable open minded people to "see again" that the true path to Jesus is one of love and acceptance.

Every week, I have people say to me: "I can no longer accept a literal interpretation of the Bible. Can I be a Christian?" Or others will say, "I'm gay, I was raised in the church and I have faith, but the church has rejected me." Or still yet, I hear: "I'm Roman Catholic. I love the church, but I can't live in its hypocrisy any longer." And with those words they all seem to say, "Teacher, let me see again." I think this piece of God's earth will be a good place for us to practice ministry, to open our eyes, and to ask with blind Bartimaeus, "Teacher, let me see again." We are surrounded by the beauty of the natural world, which ought to serve as a reminder that we are called to be good stewards of God's creation and that we must tread lightly on our physical environment to protect our often abused Mother Earth.

If you turn your eyes due east and to the immediate south, you will see neighborhoods in need of care, occupied by people who are also in need of care. We are called to serve these people who need food, clothes, and jobs. If we change direction and fix our gaze to the northwest and northeast, though we see nicer neighborhoods filled with people who have fewer physical needs and who have the capacity to serve those who are less privileged, we find them to be in desperate need of God's love. Just a few of blocks away, Crystal Bridges Museum of American Art has taken shape, an architectural wonder that holds the promise of becoming a major center of American art. With such prominent architecture bringing beauty and innovation to our neighborhood, we are compelled to pay every bit as close attention to the creation of a sacred space when we one day build our own church.

On the side of the hill to the east of where our church will be built, a family kept a garden for forty years, perhaps on the very spot where we will till the soil for a community garden that will feed the hungry. If you follow a trail down the hillside and cross over Tiger Boulevard into the hollow below, you will find a winding, spring-fed creek. This water source is a refuge from worldly concerns and serves as a place of contemplation, renewal, and prayer. The healing of blind Bartimaeus is called a miracle. Indeed, it is a miracle when people can move away from darkness and into the light, when they are gifted with the grace of "seeing again." Rudolf Bultmann wrote, "Miracle, as such, means the activity of God." It is the activity of God, the miracle of moving the communities where our churches are planted from darkness into light, that I can see happening in Bentonville on this hallowed ground. And it is to this miracle that we are all called, wherever we are. We are called in the same way that the crowd summoned blind Bartemaeus by saying, "Take heart; get up, he is calling you" (Mark 10:49).

CHAPTER 5

Creating a People

Let this be recorded for a generation yet
to come, so that a people yet unborn may
praise the LORD.

—Psalm 102:18

T he disciple Peter wanted to hold on to the notion that the
Messiah would bring victory for the Jews over their oppressors.
Instead, Jesus lived and preached a message that included suffering, death, and resurrection. When we take the time to really dig
deep into this message, it's often the resurrection part that is the most
difficult for us. This is because resurrection requires that we change.
Here in the "Bible Belt," we are very quick to adopt the job title of
"Christian." It's easy. It's the socially acceptable thing to be. However,
it's the job description that we really have trouble with. "Suffering
and death? Do I really have to lose my own life for the sake of the

gospel?" These are the difficult questions we must ponder. It's a lot easier just to show up at church on Sunday morning every once in awhile. After all, that's a very good way to keep evangelical acquaintances at bay when they ask, "Have you found a church home?"

A few years ago, much of America became hooked on the television series *Lost*. Since then, I've been trying to figure out why so many of us became *Lost* junkies. If you follow popular culture at all, you know the premise of the story. A plane, in flight from Sydney to Los Angeles, loses communication with air traffic controllers and crashes in the ocean near a beautifully idyllic and mystical deserted island. All sorts of people are on board the plane: a young doctor who is haunted by his relationship with his father; a con man; an accused murderer; a likable, morbidly obese guy who calls everybody "dude;" a wheelchair-bound cardboard-box salesman who finds that he can walk again; a woman with cancer who is healed; a rock star who is fighting his addiction to heroin; and a troubled young woman who gives birth on the island.

The common thread, and why I think we find the television series so interesting, is the opportunity that exists for all the survivors on the island to be transformed. They all bring their old lives with them, but on the island they have the chance to become something new. They all want to be saved. Everyone wants to be rescued, but if they really want to save their lives, they realize that along the way they have to be willing to give up who they were before crashing on the island.

I like to think of All Saints' as a deserted island. It is a place where one can land each Sunday morning with the same sense of hope and desperation the survivors of the *Lost* plane crash felt when they first made their way across the pure and untrodden beach sand, experiencing the opportunity for new life. As the survivors on *Lost* discover, they can't ignore who they once were. However, as long as they hold on to the baggage that they brought with them, they can't be transformed either.

After watching one episode of *Lost*, I was tempted to arrange for a dump truck to drop a few loads of fine, white sand on the parking lot in order to turn the stretch of pavement into a beach-like surface. On Sunday morning, I could imagine our parishioners pulling up their cars onto the sand-covered parking lot. I envisioned them being mystified, yet deciding to take off their shoes and socks and roll up their pants legs so they could feel the clean, unblemished sand between their toes. Every parishioner would notice how things seemed different while approaching our rented church building with a sense of expectation. They would see this red brick building floating in a sea of pure sand while watching their feet disappear below the white surface as they made their way toward the church entrance. Though every member of the church would not know quite what to expect inside, they would each have the clear sense that if they walked through the doors, they would never be quite the same.

Like the survivors of *Lost*, we have been given the opportunity to discover who we are in a new type of kinship. In the midst of a gracious and forgiving Christian community, a community that respects and encourages one another, we could embark on our quest to become something new. We at All Saints' could echo the early words of Dr. Jack Shephard in the first season, "Last week most of us were strangers and God knows how long we're going to be here. But if we can't live together we're going to die alone." It is one of the real advantages we have of being a new church. Many arrived on the shores of All Saints' not knowing another soul on the island. Walking through the deep sand, we had the chance to let go of the old self, the false self, and retain that which is good, wholesome, and true in order to allow it to flourish in an environment that was created to bring out the best that is within each of us. But the Christian life is paradoxical. If you want to save your life you must lose it. You can't hold on to the old and be something new. Those who hang on to the old life remain lost. Those who are willing to lose their old lives find life anew.

On this island that we call All Saints', it doesn't matter who you once were. It only matters who you are now. Jesus is calling us into new kinds of relationships, the type of relationships that extend beyond the legitimate and the lawful. We are called into relationships that require purity of heart, compassion, and understanding beyond a level that seems humanly possible. We are called into relationships that, if they are to succeed, require that we recognize our own need for God's mercy and an acceptance of a grace that is freely given.

The Hive Mind

For many years, I was a beekeeper. When I think of Jesus's last prayer that we may all be one, I think of the unity of spirit that is found within the beehive. This unity is expressed by the way that thousands of bees act as one. In beekeeping parlance, this unity is called the "hive mind." But actually, upon closer inspection, the "oneness" of the beehive is far more democratic (and more responsive to the individual bee) than you might imagine. When a beehive becomes too crowded, or its home becomes unsuitable for the bees living inside, scouts are sent out from the hive to look for new quarters. These scouting bees, some three to five percent, or approximately three hundred in total, will scour the countryside in search of a new home. When they find a tree with a cavity inside or a hollow wall with a narrow bee-sized entrance, they explore the potential home, sensing its size, temperature, and dryness.

Returning to the hive, the scouting bees perform a "waggle dance." The duration and enthusiasm of the scout's dance is indicative of how desirable she finds the potential new home. A great home site gets a long and vigorous "waggle dance," while the dance for a lesser quality home is shorter and less enthusiastic. Each of the hundreds of scouts, having discovered home sites of varying worth, do a "waggle dance" of corresponding duration and expression. Other bees in the hive observe the dancing bees and are drawn to the varying richness of the dances of those bees who have visited the best homes and follow them to the prospective abode. After this second wave of bees inspects the potential living space, they return to the hive and begin their own dance. They waggle vigorously if they find it to be a good place to live or, if they don't think it is very desirable, they hardly waggle at all. Eventually, the rest of the hive, responding to the dances of their fellow bees, visit the new home and dance out their own opinion. In this most democratic way, the entire hive "votes" with their little bee bodies. Acting as one, they choose a new home.

Without pressing this analogy too far, the building of community at All Saints' resembles the character of the "hive mind." Finding All Saints' to be a place where intellectual curiosity is respected, where diversity is appreciated, and where hospitality is truly practiced, our visitors signal to others through an enthusiastic sort of "waggle dance" that they may have found a home. I am grateful that enough folks have "waggle danced" in our favor, resulting in the building of a healthy and active hive.

Likewise, decision-making at All Saints' is typically done by a consensus that is similar to the "hive mind." Rarely is there a dissenting vote on issues presented to the vestry. Disagreements are usually resolved before voting takes place. And the church itself, like most organizations within the church, operates in a non-hierarchical way, without the need for dominant leadership.

Who We Are

At a monthly meeting of the vestry, I presented a draft version of a pledge card that members of our community would receive, asking them to commit to share, over the next few years, in the cost of constructing a permanent home for All Saints'. In the version I showed the vestry, there was a line that included an option to use a credit card to make future payments. As they do, the vestry thoughtfully considered the matter. At first, they focused uneasily on the logistics of handling credit cards, setting up the process with our bank, and having to manage receipts. After a few minutes of deliberation, one of the members, putting into words a concern that could already be felt throughout the room, said, "You know, I'm really not comfortable with using credit cards as a way for members to fulfill their pledge. I don't think it reflects who we are as a people. It might be okay for a megachurch, but I don't think this is All Saints'."

And another member said, "Too many people are already drawn into using credit cards and wind up having more debt than they can afford. I'm not sure we should be a part of encouraging people to get into debt."

Most of the time, the vestry meets in the library of the church that we rent from. However, when the Lutherans have a meeting or a Bible study and need the library, we pull up our chairs around a worn wooden table in the kitchen and hold our monthly meeting there. Almost as high as the altar, this table is designed for food preparation and it's particularly useful for loading bags with beans and rice to give to the hungry on Wednesday afternoons. But when a dozen or so faithful parishioners collect around the high table for a vestry meeting, its height makes us look like a group of young children assembled around a too-tall kitchen table. It almost seems as if those at the table should be armed with crayons and coloring books, intent on creating art for their mothers instead of being intent on creating solutions for the many issues vestry members typically discuss. Indeed, for adults, it's hard not to feel a little humble when you sit a table that is chest-high.

So, it was a suitable setting for me to receive a lesson in humility. I was humbled by the wisdom of the vestry. While I had been thinking about how best to collect money and more about logistics and ease of payment, the vestry reminded me of who we really are and what we are called to do. I could tell by the expressions on their faces and the nods around the room that the vestry was "in full accord and of one mind," "having the same love," and "looking not to their own interests, but to the interests of others" (Phil. 2:2, 4). The vestry understood that there was no reason for the church to be yet another place that tempts us to live beyond our means. The Apostle Paul would have certainly agreed.

Psychologist Roy F. Baumeister and the scientific writer John Tierney have coauthored a book titled *Willpower*. In this book, they both contend that willpower, whether it's the ability to say no to a chocolate cupcake or the capacity to "look not to your own interests, but to the interests of others," is like a muscle that can be strengthened with exercise or fatigued with overuse. In the short term, they believe that willpower is a limited resource, so it should be used sparingly. However, in the long run and with practice, they propose that our willpower can be strengthened and our capacity to do what we already know is right and good for ourselves and others can increase. In a community, in a place where members have agreed among themselves to lift one another up, there is luxurious space to allow the muscles of compassion and sympathy to be flexed. We can let go of selfish ambition and conceit in an atmosphere in which it is safe to do so. In this space, you have every reason to expect that you will not be alone in striving to cultivate a sense of humility and self-emptying. At its very best, the church is a training ground, a school of love.

All Saints' is the kind of community in which we can be strengthened by association with one another. It is a place where we are called to imitate the Christ and a place where we can be ourselves. It is a space where we can be true to the faith we profess and, at the same time, remain true to who we really are. Imitation of the Christ is not pretense; it isn't dressing up on Sunday morning and putting on a sanctimonious attitude. Rather, imitation of the Christ is allowing that which is best within you, that which is good, holy, and right, to rise up to the surface.

Common Faith, Uncommon Belief

One of our parishioners told me of an experience he had while at a church one Sunday in which the priest asked that everyone in the congregation, during the reading of the Nicene Creed, stand at the reciting of the portions of the Creed that they agreed with and sit at the parts of the Creed with which they disagreed. Everyone stood as the Creed began: "We believe in one God. . . " but on the second line when the congregation read, "the Father," a few people sat down because their relationships with their biological fathers had been troublesome and they didn't like to think of God as a father figure. As the congregation read "the Almighty," a few others sat down since their conception of God wasn't of a deity who was all-powerful. Others sat at "maker of heaven and earth," because they had studied science and they couldn't reconcile what they knew about astrophysics and evolution with what a literal reading of Genesis teaches about the creation of the world.

Most stood for "God from God, Light from Light, true God from true God," because they didn't know exactly what to disagree with there. Some couldn't imagine that Jesus "became incarnate from the Virgin Mary," so they took their seats. Others were skeptical of Jesus's resurrection on the third day, so they sat down when it came to that part of the creed. Most everyone stood to read, "We believe in one holy catholic and apostolic church," because if they didn't believe in church, they wouldn't have been there. Finally, in anticipation of "the life of the world to come" the entire congregation stood, because in varying ways everyone gathered on that particular morning professed a hope for some kind of new life.

We bring with us our own meanings behind what we profess we believe. We can interpret creeds and prayers and scripture in widely divergent ways and hold in our minds and hearts very different conceptions of the way God works in our world. Yet each Sunday, we stand together, side by side, and say words that signal to those around us that we are all children of God, we are united by love and respect for one another, and we are a people joined together, not by mere belief, but by a common faith.

Divine Alchemy

After church one Sunday, one of our parishioners walked up the stairs to my office. I was expecting a characteristically light-hearted comment on my sermon since he was smiling as usual, but something was different this time. His face was glowing, perhaps even radiant. He said to me: "You know, something happened to me during communion today. I realized that we are part of something really big." I had heard that comment before. In fact, I had heard it earlier that same day when two long-time members made a similar statement before the church service began, sharing the realization that we were growing far beyond the intrepid band of misfits that had gathered for our first service in the auditorium at Washington Junior High School. But my office visitor, with his face aglow, meant something completely different. "I realized," he said, "that this isn't just about me. We're all connected. We're all together in this. All of us."

It was a classic moment of movement in the direction, as our Buddhist friends would understand it, of enlightenment and of realization, not just on an intellectual level, but with an understanding of the heart. Indeed, we are all connected, we are all One, and we are all apiece with Creation. In the language of Christianity, it is the Holy Spirit that moves among us, weaving her way in and through us, binding us and keeping us together.

The Body of Christ

In his letter to the people of Corinth, the Apostle Paul uses the body, the actual physical body, as a way of depicting the membership in the body of Christ, specifically the early Christian community. Paul wasn't the first in the Greco-Roman world of which he was a part to use the body as way of understanding human community. He did, however, offer a rather different take on the structure. Instead of thinking of the body in a hierarchical way, designating the head or the heart or the liver as the most important parts of the body, Paul recognized that every component in the body plays a vital role in the well-being of the whole. No part is greater than another. Indeed, as Paul wrote, "God has so arranged the body, giving the greater honor to the inferior member, that there may be no dissension within the body" (1 Cor 12:24–25). No one member is greater than any other, no matter his or her gifts.

If we think of the church as a body, as Paul suggests, what part of the body do you think you would be? Are you the hands of the church? When something needs to be done are you quick to roll up your sleeves, get your hands dirty, and get it done? Or are you the church's strong shoulders? Are you someone that others can lean on for support? Perhaps you are the ears that listen patiently. Do you make sure that other voices are truly heard? Maybe you are the eyes that possess a clear vision of where we are headed as a people. Are you the legs that can run with an idea? Or are you the knees that kneel in prayer, asking for God's mission here to be accomplished? Maybe you are the brain that can devise a plan and implement a strategy to accomplish that mission. Are you the compassionate heart that pumps the lifeblood through our congregation? Perhaps you are the voice that is lifted in songs of praise and thanksgiving or offers wise counsel. You might be the funny bone that makes sure we never take ourselves too seriously. Perhaps you are the loving arms that understand our body's particular kind of hospitality and so you embrace the stranger and the unloved.

We are all part of the body of Christ; every component of that body is important. But I have an embarrassing confession to make. The part of my own body that causes me the most concern is my feet. My feet are a mess. I've been running on them for half a century and they look like it. My feet are flat; they have bunions, corns, and calluses. My toes point in odd directions. I have even had a stone bruise on my left heel. My feet often ache, they turn cold easily, they complain constantly. While they demand an inordinate amount of attention, they carry me everywhere I go.

Some members of the body of Christ are like my feet. They are in pain, they are in need, they are wounded, they have been abused, they cry out for attention, and they are troubled and even sometimes troublesome. Even so, they carry us forward and they provide us with an opportunity to practice care, generosity, and understanding. By our reaction to their need, they tell us who we are as a people of God and how we are progressing on the path toward becoming a people of compassion. They are our troublesome teachers, essential members of the body of Christ. In seminary, I can remember my professor of pastoral care advising me to keep in mind that everyone I encounter in the parish is wounded. Everyone is wounded, even the most arrogant, confident, and self-assured. We are the walking wounded and "made to drink of one Spirit."

The real picture of the body of Christ is a little more complex. There is really no clear division between the parts of the body in need and those healthier parts that can address the need. Paul tells us that ". . . all the members of the body, though many, are one, and so it is with Christ" (1 Cor. 12:12). We must always remember that we are all connected; when we show kindness to those that are wounded or suffer, we are being kind to ourselves as well.

An important component of Dr. Edwin Friedman's family systems theory is the idea of "self-differentiation." This is the process of learning how to remain connected to those around you, those you love, and at the same time, separating yourself from them in a way that allows you to become an autonomous, self-nurturing individual. A differentiated person can be intensely involved in the lives of others, while at the same time not allow himself or herself to get too caught up in the problems and opinions of others.

The Apostle Paul was definitely a family systems theorist. As Paul wrote to the Corinthians, "If one member suffers, all suffer together with it; if one member is honored, all rejoice together with it." Paul's statement raises all kinds of interesting questions for us as a people of God. How can I develop a close relationship with you and still stay true to the person that I am? How can I show genuine compassion for others and yet not be overwhelmed by their own suffering? How can I take pleasure in the achievements of another person, find joy in his or her victories, and not become jealous?

A church is a really good place to practice that kind of self-differentiation. Most relationships at the workplace are too formal, too fleeting, or even too distant to allow you to practice achieving any real, substantial self-differentiation. Family relationships, in which people live within the same emotional skin, can be so intense and so close, that in the beginning stages of becoming a self-differentiated individual, it is all too easy to fall into old patterns of absorbing the anxiety swirling around you and react without thinking.

However, a church, if you are willing to be involved in it, can provide a safe place to practice being separate parts of the same body. At its very best, church can be a place where we accept an appropriate level of responsibility for each other, a place where conformity isn't expected and where differences can be celebrated. Church is a place where, in relationship with others, we can most fully be who we really are; where our interconnectedness as a community of Christ creates and molds our truest self. "For in the one Spirit we were all baptized into one body" (1 Cor. 12:13).

CHAPTER 6

Shaping a People

The gifts he gave were that some would be apostles, some prophets, some evangelists, some pastors and teachers, to equip the saints for the work of ministry, for building up the body of Christ.

—Ephesians 4:11–12

In July 2007, when we met for the last time in the auditorium at Washington Junior High School, I preached the following sermon:

> After this the Lord appointed seventy others and sent them on ahead of him in pairs to every town and place where he himself intended to go. He said to them, "The harvest is plentiful, but the laborers

are few" (Luke 10:1–2). If all goes as planned, today will be our last Sunday meeting at Washington Junior High School. Next Sunday, we will meet for the first time at Christ the King Lutheran Church. Our journey will only be about a mile and a half up Central Avenue. And I don't think that by making our next temporary home in the midst of the Lutherans we will feel like lambs in the middle of a pack of wolves. In fact, I expect our welcome to be warm, gracious, and sincere.

However, if Garrison Keilor's frequent characterizations of Lutherans are to be believed, our welcome may be just a little more than subdued. As an example, take this stanza from a Prairie Home Companion anthem titled "I'm a Lutheran:"

Once in awhile we go to shows
But a Lutheran is not a fan.
We don't whistle and we don't laugh
We smile as loud as we can.
If you come to church, don't expect to be hugged,
Don't expect your hand to be shook.
If we need to know who you are,
We can look in the visitors book.
Now I have nothing against Episcopalians.
I believe in an open door.
I'm sure it's good to get new ideas.
But we never did it that way before.

We will have much to learn. There may be a few fits and starts. But this experience will form us. We will learn how we worship, how we "are" in a setting that is actually designed for worship. And we will learn from the Lutherans. Perhaps we will learn directly from joint education classes and shared liturgies, but more importantly, we will learn how to share a space and how we can work together. In many ways, this is similar to the way that newly wed spouses learn to live together.

As the reading from Luke suggests, our provisions will be light. And so, we will leave behind the pulpit, lectern, altar, and bishop's chair that we wrestle into place each Sunday morning. Jesus tells us to eat and drink what is provided for us. We don't know what form of sustenance we are going to receive, but it will be provided and it will nourish us.

In this passage, Jesus has constructed a "second sending." This sending is not just of the original twelve, but of about seventy disciples that have been commissioned to go ahead together to prepare the way for Jesus. I think this move to Christ the King Church is our "second sending." We already count more than seventy among our band of believers, but that's not far from the usual number of us that show up on any given Sunday. It fills me with wonder about what our "second sending" will be like. We are a people being prepared, a people in forma-tion, a people being transformed for the work of the kingdom. And we are being sent forth to con-tinue the process of change in order to become God's people.

As he sent them forth, Jesus said the following to the seventy disciples: "Carry no purse, no bag, no sandals" (Luke 10:4). He instructed them to travel light. Last week, I asked Bishop Benfield what we should do with our altar furniture. He responded by saying, "Return it to the diocese so that we can use it for the next church plant." I like that idea. I like the idea of using the furniture for a short period of time and then passing it on to a new mission. I like the idea of All Saints' learning to stand on its own two feet sooner than expected and also its playing a role in supporting the planting of other mission churches.

I had intended to rent a small storage space here in Bentonville and move our altar furniture there. This was my attempt to hedge our bets in case our "sending forth" to the land of the Lutherans didn't work out as planned. But Jesus's admonition to travel light, not to mention the bishop's instructions, have persuaded me that when a people receive a commission to go forth, a back-up plan isn't required.

Bishop Benfield was thrilled with the energy and vitality that he sensed among us last Sunday. In conversation with those being received and confirmed into the church, it was evident to him that something exciting was happening here, but he offered me a caveat. He recalled how another new Episcopal church, having met in a movie theatre for some time, finally moved into their own worship space. It was a time of great rejoicing and of no small amount of relief. However, a funny thing happened; the energy went out of the congregation. While they met in the theatre, the energy of the people had been directed at setting up the worship space, having church in a temporary setting, and then dismantling the space Sunday after Sunday. The move to a more stable location left the congregants with no place to channel their energy and no focus for their attention.

I don't really fear this for a church like All Saints'. Especially if we take seriously the observation that Jesus gave the seventy disciples in their "second sending." Just like the seventy, we are being sent on our way and we have plenty to keep us busy: "The harvest is plentiful, but the laborers are few" (Luke 10:2). While we will stop moving furniture around, there remains even more important work to be done. Almost everyone here has a job in the church; everyone is involved in some aspect of creating worship on Sunday mornings. If it's not moving furniture, then it's putting up signs, preparing food, reading the lessons, designing the bulletin, leading Godly Play, creating our music, greeting guests, serving as acolytes or chalice bearers, and the list goes on and on. Sometimes, I wonder how we even find renewal in worship with so much work going on.

As most of you know, I recently spent twelve days training with the Congregational Development Institute in Seattle. One of the things we talked a great deal about was the Apostolate-Renewal cycle. The model envisions a congregational life in which parishioners are renewed by the experience of church. The liturgy, the music, the prayers, and the fellowship that take place on Sunday morning are intended to renew, invigorate, and bring freshness into the lives of those who attend. But this renewal has a purpose to form us and to equip us for the ministry that takes place beyond the walls of the sanctuary. The apostolate side of the model recognizes that we are called to the work of the kingdom, which includes healing the sick, feeding the poor, and bringing the peace of Christ into every home and business we enter.

As a church plant with a developing congregation, the cycle is a little muddled. The work we do is primarily centered on the creation of a worship service. With our move into the Christ the King Church, this means that some of that workload will lighten. As we continue to grow, the burden of all the kinds of work that is involved in creating worship can be spread among a larger group of parishioners. The process of creating a Sunday morning worship service will get a little easier. As that happens, I expect that church will become a place where we can more readily find renewal. Indeed, with our move into a consecrated holy space, a setting that has been prayed in, around, and through for decades, the renewal of spirit we all seek on Sunday mornings will happen with a little less labor and a little more naturally.

If folks arrive early enough on Sunday mornings at Washington Junior High School, they witnessed the miraculous process where, with the shifting of a few pieces of furniture and by laying out of a few altar hangings, a school auditorium was transformed into a sacred place. With the move to Christ the King Church, my hope for the transformation that takes place on Sunday mornings would become less about moving furniture around and more about transforming our very selves, rearranging our hearts, shifting our souls, and changing our minds, thus equipping the people of All Saints' for the work of Christ in the world.

Spiritual Semites

The biblical scholar and spiritual retreat leader Lynn Bauman teaches that we are "spiritual Semites." We Christians, together with Jews and Muslims, are part of the Abrahamic tradition. All three religions trace their origins back to Abraham, Sarah, and Hagar. Abraham and his descendants were nomadic desert people and they were shaped by the geography of the Middle East. The arid nature of the landscape meant that these people were compelled to be constantly on the move. When the rains ceased and the grass disappeared, they packed their tents and gathered their livestock and moved on in search of green pastures. To stay in one place and to remain stationary was to choose death. So the people moved from the oasis, to the desert, back to the oasis, and back to the desert again. It was a constant cycle; they were always searching for a place they could make their home.

The Exodus story is emblematic of this pattern. After finding slavery in Egypt no longer bearable, Moses led the Israelites across the Reed Sea, into the deserts of Sinai, and eventually into the fertile hills and plains of Palestine. The actual journey, if one were to walk as the Israelites did from Egypt to Palestine, would take about two weeks. However, the Israelites wandered in the desert for forty years before arriving at their home. This incredible length of time was not because they got lost or wandered in circles, but because they simply were not ready. In the desert, they were undergoing a process of formation. The Israelites were being formed as God's people; they were finding their identity and learning who they were.

Though the congregation of All Saints' may live in the fertile valleys and green hills of Northwest Arkansas, it is possible to remain a desert people, in the spiritual sense. The land is purchased and the congregation has had a taste of what it's like to worship on the "Promised Land." Everyone is beginning to ask the same question: "When are we going to build the church?" I can hear an eagerness in everyone's voices, myself included, to move quickly through the desert land toward the oasis. At the same time, I have to wonder that if a generous soul were to drop a few million dollars in the offering plate one Sunday morning, would All Saints' be ready? I'm not asking if the site plan is complete, if the architect's drawings are done, or even if sufficient input has been gathered from all our outreach, education, and worship ministries. I'm asking if All Saints' has done the "soul work" that is necessary. Have the people of All Saints' spent sufficient time in the desert for self-discovery? And has their identity as a people of God been revealed to them? In short, is All Saints' sufficiently formed? In the life of All Saints' this period of time between now and when construction on the building begins is necessary for formation, to make this church ready to fully receive God's abundant grace.

When the disciples ask Jesus, "How is it that you will reveal yourself to us?" (John 14:22), Jesus tells them to keep his word and to keep his words. But there is more to his instruction than an admonition to keep the commandments or to follow Jesus's example. Jesus implores his disciples that when he is gone from them, the Father will send in his name an Advocate, which is the Holy Spirit, who will continue to teach and remind them of all that Jesus said.

All Saints' is currently at the threshold of embarkation, the beginning of a process of finding the way home and of creating a new home. Christ's promise is that if we love him, he and the Father will make their home with us. And it is in that process of making a home for the Father, the Son, and the Holy Spirit, that the people of All Saints' have been and will continue to be transformed.

Our Stories

One of the great benefits of being a priest is the privilege of learning the stories of our members. Whenever someone new comes to All Saints', I usually arrange to have coffee or lunch with them so that I can hear their story and learn something about what brought them to us and how we can be of service to them. Sometimes, the stories gush out like water over a spillway. Other times, the stories are revealed more slowly as time passes and trust develops. But I've learned that we all have a story, usually with a back-story, which is often richly layered with story upon story. It is our collection of stories, our shared stories, that forms a community.

The story that lies within the story is always intriguing. If you walk into All Saints' and stay for coffee hour, it doesn't take long to learn something of our parish story. It is a story of how we began meeting in the auditorium at Washington Junior High School and how we now share space with the Lutherans at Christ the King

Church. It is also a rich narrative that explains why we opened our arms to every member in the community, especially those who were not received well elsewhere. It's an account that charts how we have grown gradually over the years, purchased land, and are now committed to building a beautiful sacred space. But there is another story at a deeper level that speaks to the smaller groups and guilds that make up All Saints', that is, the community within the community. Still deeper, there are the many interesting and complicated individual narratives that make up our collective story.

Barbara Brown Taylor says that what the writer of Mark is doing with the stories he tells is establishing Jesus's identity. Taylor writes, "They are not stories about how to get God to do what we want, which is just another way of trying to stay in control. Instead, they are stories about who God is, and how God acts, and what God is like." Our own prayers for healing may or may not be answered in the way that we ask for them to be answered. As Michael Lindvall has written, ". . . prayer is not simply a matter of bending the vector of divine will toward my needs, and my hopes. Rather, when we ask something of God, the act of asking moves us into closer relationship with God. Our prayer may or may not change God's mind, but our own hearts and minds will be changed by the encounter." God works with us in this project of bringing healing to the world. The power that Jesus exercises is relational power. The faith that the hemorrhaging woman brought with her into her encounter with the Christ was a faith that was made apparent in her willingness to step out of the crowd. She reaches to touch Jesus's garments and Jesus calls her to step out; she became the instrument of her own healing.

We are called to be co-creators and agents of change with God. God's power has often been portrayed in the tradition as coercive, omnipotent, unchanging, and unaffected by the world. But as co-creators, we are called to share power with God, to fully engage in the unfolding drama of life that is influenced by the presence of God in relationship with us. Frederick Buechner writes that Jesus is speaking to us as he did to Jairus's daughter, telling us to rise up and live: "You who believe, and you who sometimes believe and sometimes don't believe much of anything, and you who would give almost anything to believe if only you could, 'Get up,' he says, all of you—all of you!" Jesus gives life not only to the dead, but to those of us who are "only partly alive. . . who much of the time live with our lives closed to the wild beauty and the miracle of things, including the wild beauty and miracle of every day we live and even of ourselves." This is the power at the heart of the common story we all believe and of all the stories that we live: "the power of new life, new hope, new being."

From Acorns to Oaks

Jesus is often teaching his disciples a lesson that requires an alternative way of thinking about the world, a transformation of consciousness. A transformed consciousness isn't something that can be shared. Alternative ways of thinking have to be created anew within each of us. Consciousness cannot be given away or received as a donation. We are all called to an awakening from our slumber, a realization that we are more than the world tells us we are. If the Divine Light that is within us is to truly shine, it must be nourished and cultivated.

Cynthia Bourgeault, an Episcopal priest, tells this story:

> Once upon a time, in a not-so-far-away land, there was a kingdom of acorns nestled at the foot of a grand old oak tree. Since the citizens of this kingdom were modern, fully Westernized acorns, they went about their business with purposeful energy; and since they were midlife, baby-boomer acorns, they engaged in a lot of self-help courses. There were seminars called "Getting All You Can out of Your Shell." There were woundedness and recovery groups for acorns who had been bruised in their original fall from the tree.

There were spas for oiling and polishing those shells and various acorn-opathic therapies to enhance longevity and well-being.

One day in the midst of this kingdom, there suddenly appeared a knotty little stranger, apparently dropped "out of the blue" by a passing bird. He was capless and dirty, making an immediate negative impression on his fellow acorns. And couched beneath the oak tree, he stammered out a wild tale. Pointing upward at the tree, he said, "We . . . are . . . that!"

Delusional thinking, obviously, the other acorns concluded, but one of them continued to engage him in conversation: "So tell us, how would we become that tree?"

"Well," said he, pointing downward, "it has something to do with going into the ground . . . and cracking open the shell."

"Insane," they responded. "Totally morbid! Why, then, we wouldn't be acorns anymore!"

For Christians, baptism is the beginning of a transformative experience, a symbolic movement into the earth beneath the waters of baptism. The water that splashes from the pitcher into the font and flows from the priest's hand onto the baptismal candidate's head is representative of the living waters necessary for each of us to grow into the fully realized human beings we are meant to be.

There are sound theological and pastoral reasons to baptize infants. Baptizing is a way of welcoming a child into the church, into a community of faithful people. It's a way of marking the infant as Christ's own, as a child of God. Furthermore, it gives notice to parents, godparents, and the gathered congregation alike that the precious nature and divine attributes of the child have been entrusted to our collective care. In addition, there is something beautiful about allowing the living waters of the Divine Spirit to rain down on this tiny acorn of a child. Receiving baptism before a hard shell has formed from the pain, disappointment, and hard knocks of life is a grace unlike any other. Without that hard shell, the living waters can more easily find their way into the germinating seed of a soul contained within a child's tiny body. When we grow older, a fall is often required, to break open that protective shell, so the waters of Christ can seep in. It is my prayer that when we witness the waters of baptism nourishing a newly born child, that we may also be born anew and in the renewal of our baptismal vows rediscover who we really are. This baptismal rebirth and renewal is such a vital task when forming the identity of any newly planted church community.

Emmanuel

Every child could be named Emmanuel, for with the birth of each new child comes the blessed assurance that God is always with us. The community of All Saints' is full of children. Occasionally, we will have them sing and sign songs before the congregation, such as "Give Thanks With a Grateful Heart." At the annual Christmas pageant, the children gather in front of the congregation cast as Mary and Joseph, the wise men, the angels, and the sheep in order to re-tell the story of Jesus's birth. More than actors and actresses in mere performances, these children are vibrant, life-filled reminders of the presence of the Holy Spirit. The children of a church are the flesh and bone evidence of Emmanuel, that God is with us.

Standing on the chancel, the children re-tell the Christmas story. Not only is this story remembered by having the children narrate and beautifully portray the characters found in every manger scene, but their radiant faces and youthful bodies convey more of a sense of Advent than all the songs and sermons I could imagine. In the faces of children, we see a rainbow collection of children whose parents come from all classes, races, and creeds. They are the children of parents without the documents that would make their residency status, or their union with each other, "legal" in the eyes of the law. Even still, moments like these so clearly reveal to us that all are God's children. In these children's faces could be seen the hope and the expectation of a brighter, more compassionate future for all humankind. All Saints' is a small child of a church as well. Healthy, vibrant, and newborn, the word is spreading about the birth of All Saints'. To live into its reputation, All Saints', and any other new church plant, would do well to imitate children, to convey to the world in every way possible the same spirit of Advent that these children have taught us. All of us are called into a series of new relationships with God, our neighbors, and those we love and those we haven't yet learned to love.

We worship a God who wants to bring us all into relationship, a God whose radical act at Christmas was to provide us with a living, breathing example of what it means for God to walk on earth. The promise of God is found in the loving relationships with everyone we encounter and its fulfillment is embodied in the name Emmanuel. God is always with us.

Identity

I like to imagine All Saints' as a place where a person can discover their true identity. A place where you can let go of the false sense of self learned from sources as disparate as cruel stepfathers and slick advertisers, all peddlers of a false gospel. I imagine a place where we can learn and practice what it means to serve others, rather than devoting our entire lives to the accumulation of goods. The quest for identity reminds me of the story of the Baptist, the Catholic, and the Episcopalian who arrive at the gates of heaven, where they meet Jesus. Jesus tells them that before they enter he wants them to answer one question: "Who do you say that I am?"

The Baptist begins, "Well, the Bible says. . . "

Jesus says, "I didn't ask what the Bible says, I asked who do *you* say."

The Catholic gives it a try: "The Church teaches. . . "

Jesus, becoming a little impatient, says, "I didn't ask about the Church, I asked *you*."

The Episcopalian says, "You are the Christ, the son of the Living God."

Jesus smiles. "Yes," he says, "thank you."

The Episcopalian continues, saying, "But, on the other hand. . . "

A central question faces today's Christian: What do Jesus's words have to say to you? How are you, as a member of the contemporary church and as a practitioner of an established religion, able to come to terms with the prospect of following a radical, countercultural first-century prophet whose message was aimed at liberation, freedom, and lifting up the lowly?

What does Jesus have to say to us? At its heart, Jesus's message was a call for personal and communal transformation. If you are content with the status quo, if you are satisfied with your life and with the state of the world, then the notion of picking up a cross and following Jesus and giving up all that you have in order to be a disciple is not likely to have much appeal. But if you are seeking transformation, if you hunger to know God in a radical, life-altering way, if there is an emptiness inside you that can't be filled with all the possessions you can pile on, then maybe Jesus's words, even at their most severe and strident, will hit home. And nothing will ever be the same again.

A New Thing

God has chosen this place, Bentonville, Arkansas, and called the people of All Saints', in order to do a new thing. Self-described mythologist, Devutt Pattanaik, tells the story of a fourth-century encounter between the Greek conqueror of nations, Alexander the Great, and a naked wise man in India called a gymnosophist. Alexander the Great approached the gymnosophist, who was sitting on a rock and simply staring up at the sky. Alexander asked him, "So what are you doing?"

The gymnosophist answered, "I'm experiencing nothingness." Then the gymnosophist asked, "What are you doing?"

And Alexander said, "I am conquering the world."

And they both laughed. Each one thought the other was a fool. The gymnosophist thought, "Why is he conquering the world? It's pointless." And Alexander thought, "Why is he sitting around doing nothing? What a waste of a life."

As Christians, we are called by God to occupy something of a middle ground between the worldview of Alexander the Great and that of the naked wise man. Scripture repeatedly calls us to action, but to contemplation as well. We are called into an alliance to help accomplish God's work in the world. At the same time, we are to seek the God within, in stillness, prayer, and reflection. The Christian path is a path of formation, not simply of destination. God is shaping us through the work we are called to do. God forms us, not just as individuals, but as a people, to accomplish God's purpose.

If that is so, what is God's purpose? What is that new thing that God is about to do at a progressive church plant such as All Saints'? The New International Version puts Isaiah's prophecy firmly into the present tense, "See, I am doing a new thing! Now it springs up; do you not perceive it?" There are two very obvious ways in which God has been doing a new thing in our midst. The first is apparent to most every visitor who walks in our doors. We are an unusually hospitable people. Over and over again, I am told by visitors how welcome they have felt at All Saints'. And we don't just welcome the bright-eyed young couple who look like they could be recruited to teach a Sunday school class or the well-heeled executive whose tithe would ensure the success of a stewardship campaign. We also welcome those who are ignored or shunned in other places. Our brand of radical hospitality is indeed a very new thing.

The second thing that God is doing at All Saints' is creating a remarkably inclusive community. If we were able to gather the All Saints' parishioners who attend all three of our services into one place, there would be no other church in Benton County where a more diverse collection of God's children are assembled. The complexion of our faces reflects the colors of the rainbow, we are young and old, we are rich and poor, the varied sexual orientations and gender identities and expressions of our congregation reflect God's delight in the immense diversity of creation. As Isaiah prophesied, the Lord "shall arbitrate for many peoples" (Isa. 2:4). It is an ancient prophesy, but in this time and place, it is something new.

God isn't done with us. God is about to do more new things. I don't pretend to know exactly what God has in store for us, but let me suggest a couple of possibilities. As God desired for Zion, God wants us to beat our swords into plowshares and our spears into pruning hooks. I recognize that not many of us are in a position to have much influence on how war is waged or whether nation shall "lift up sword against nation." But we do have the capacity to practice peace. The demanding environment in which we live often makes it difficult for us to let go of tension once the workday has ended. We bring the pressure and tightness of that world into our homes and into our churches. I envision a day when every church is known as a place of peace, of letting go, as sanctuaries wherein one breathes more easily and leaves the tensions of the world behind.

Second, I envision church as a place that understands that we are called by God not simply to engage in charitable acts, but to work for social justice as well. We are generous in offering alms to the poor, ensuring that people are fed and that no one is without a warm coat on a winter's night. But when we live in a place in which the disparity in wealth is great, we cannot turn a blind eye to inequality. Something is badly wrong when abject poverty exists in the midst of such plenty. God's call for justice for all people will require that as a community of the faithful, we will become a voice crying in the wilderness on behalf of the voiceless. And it will be something new. May the God of Jacob teach us his ways, that we may walk in his paths: "Let us walk in the light of the LORD" (Isa. 2:5).

CHAPTER 7

It Looks Like the Kingdom of God

Again I saw that under the sun the race is not to the swift, nor the battle to the strong, nor bread to the wise, nor riches to the intelligent, nor favor to the skillful, but time and chance happen to them all.

—Ecclesiastes 9:11

Jesus put before the crowd another parable: "The kingdom of heaven may be compared to someone who sowed good seed in his field; but while everybody was asleep, an enemy came and sowed weeds among the wheat, and then went away. So when the plants came up and bore grain, then the weeds appeared as well. And the slaves of the householder came and said to him, 'Master, did you not sow good seed in your field? Where, then, did these weeds come from?'" (Matt. 13:24–27).

I will admit that I have a certain partiality toward weeds. If you look from the back of our house down the hillside leading to the water, you won't find a neatly manicured lawn or the sterile uniformity of stone landscaping popular in Bella Vista. What you will see is an abundance of native grasses, an odd assortment of flowering plants, aspiring pine trees, thistles, vines, and all varieties of ground cover. A winding path makes its way through this collection of "natural landscaping," what my next-door neighbors call "a buncha weeds."

I think my affinity toward weeds began when I was on the waning edge of adolescence and my Dad decided there were too many useless plants growing in our cow pasture. He realized that he could simultaneously deal with the problem of an excess amount of rangy, quickly growing, almost out-of-hand weeds, as well as a son of a similar nature. So, he armed me with leather gloves and a sharpened hoe and pointed me in the direction of the bull nettles.

The particular weed my Dad had in mind has the scientific name, *Cnidoscolus texanus*. In Spanish, the weed is called *mala mujer*, which translates into English as "bad woman." Prickly pear is better known, more prolific, and deserving of its reputation as a plant to be reckoned with. On the other hand, bull nettle is more sinister. It doesn't need much moisture; the hotter the weather, the happier it is. Its beauty belies its threat. The stalks have thorns, but the dark green leaves are the real problem. The top and underside of each leaf contain thousands of tiny hair-like thorns, each waiting to inject a caustic juice into the skin of the unwary. The poison doesn't act immediately. If you inadvertently brush your skin against the leaves, there is a slight prickly sensation followed by a few seconds of impending doom as the body's pain receptors begin to send a signal to the brain that agony is on the way. As with much of life, the waiting for pain is actually worse than the pain itself. Nevertheless, the pain from bull nettles is real, causing burning, stinging, and itching for hours.

The stand of bull nettle dotted the pasture below our house, as far in the distance as I could see. I worked among the nettles every morning for several weeks. I chopped at the stalks, attempted to pull up as many of the roots as I could, and hoped that the plants wouldn't reappear with the next rainfall. What struck me the most was that the deep green of each plant was punctuated by the presence of a dozen small white flowers. Each flower had three petals as if to make a tiny trinity among the thorns. The scent of the blooms was slightly sweet and subtle, carrying a memory of spring across the browning summer grass. Each petal was eventually pushed aside by the emergence of a small white nut, which I soon discovered contained three kernels. The nut was difficult to retrieve and I was stung more than once as I learned the art of carefully extracting the seed from the leafy guards that surrounded each nut. Breaking through the hard shell required a hammer or pliers, but the sweetness of each morsel made the danger and effort worthwhile. Perhaps it was the risk and the work that made the nut so delectable.

Despite wearing boots, jeans, a long-sleeved shirt, and gloves, it was inevitable that I would occasionally be bitten by bull nettle. The folk remedy Dad suggested for the sting, applying a poultice of mud pulled from the clay bottom of the nearby stock tank, proved effective. Though now I can see that leaving my sweat-soaked clothes on the shore and plunging into the cooling waters of the tank was just the distraction I needed from the stinging whelps and the seemingly endless labor. At morning's end, I would survey my work and see a hundred wilting plants, lying on their sides and disarmed, like so many fallen soldiers. It was a crumpled collection of flowers and fruit and prickly armor.

We would be hard pressed to find a wheat field today that resembles the one that Jesus describes in this parable of the wheat and the weeds. Weeds are almost nonexistent in the modern wheat field. Instead, there is acre upon acre of sameness, hybrid versions of plants with resistance to weeds and disease built into their genetic structure, and herbicides that make it virtually impossible for a weed to appear in row after row of monoculture. In order to maximize yield per acre and to take advantage of current high grain prices, diversity is eliminated on the modern farm and the wheat is planted so close to houses that a farm laborer can reach out his bedroom window and touch the grain. Neither the laborer nor the owner needs to worry about uprooting the wheat while gathering the weeds. The weeds can't even find a place to take root.

Beyond the wheat field, the world is, thankfully, still a more diverse and interesting place. The lowly weed, the unwanted plant, is free to find its way along with the rest of the botanical kingdom. By definition, a weed is an unwanted plant. Take for example a majestic oak in the path of a shopping mall or even a rosebush in the wheat field. Jesus makes it clear in this parable that in the kingdom he envisions, our task isn't about uprooting weeds. The separation of the weeds from the wheat is clearly not our work. When we pull the weeds, we not only do damage to the wheat, but we also destroy the unrealized potential of the weed including its flower, its fruit, and its fragrance.

Besides, I'm not sure we would know how to distinguish weed from wheat anyway. And when I consider the good folks that make up All Saints', and especially when I look in the mirror at myself, I see a lot of weediness. And so, we live with our weeds. We are stung by them, fascinated by them, fed by them, have our nostrils filled with their perfume. Our lives are made richer because of their presence; it's the bountiful harvest of a church that seeks diversity in a culture that dictates conformity.

A parable like this offers us the freedom to go about the business of being planters and of not having to worry so much about who belongs in the kingdom. We can go around looking for weeds or we can get on with the business of growing wheat. This is the liberating, fulfilling, and absolutely thrilling business of growing, becoming, and not judging. We are part of the project of blessing all creation and freed from the task of deciding who merits God's blessing. Indeed, we are a collection of beautiful weeds. Our flowers, our fruit, and even our thorns are what make us beautiful and true and cause us to shine like the sun in the kingdom of our Father. Let us bless the harvest.

A Fig Tree in the Vineyard

Jesus told this parable: "A man had a fig tree planted in his vineyard; and he came looking for fruit on it and found none. So he said to the gardener, 'See here! For three years I have come looking for fruit on this fig tree, and still I find none. Cut it down! Why should it be wasting the soil?' He replied, 'Sir, let it alone for one more year, until I dig around it and put manure on it. If it bears fruit next year, well and good; but if not, you can cut it down.'" (Luke 13:6–9)

The fig tree is growing in the middle of the vineyard and probably holding up the grape vines, but it's not producing fruit. It is this absence of fruit that is the topic of conversation between the landowner and the gardener. There are a number of reasons why a fig tree might not bear fruit. It could be too young. Shoots from a fig tree are typically sprouted in pots for two or three years before they are planted in land. Then, it can take up to two years after it is planted before it can be expected to produce fruit. Thus, fruit could only be anticipated on the tree's fourth, fifth, or even sixth year.

Nevertheless, a fig tree is quite resilient. Even if it is cut down it can be counted on to grow back. However, it does require special care if it is to be truly productive and bear fruit. The Hellenistic agricultural manuals suggest rich, humid soil and manure around the base of the tree. Watering is recommended when the fruit is swelling, but the soil is to be left relatively dry otherwise.

At the end of the discussion about what to do with the fruitless fig tree, the gardener recommends to the landowner that he dig around the base of the tree and add manure. Apparently, during the early years of the fig tree's life the two had done nothing to properly care for the young tree.

So, we might think of this parable as the story of two flawed farmers. The vintner was into his third year of coming to the fig tree in search of figs. When he finds no figs growing on the tree, his first impulse is to cut it down. However, in the two previous years the gardener had done nothing to enrich the soil, ensure that it was pruned properly, or even watered at the appropriate times of the year. The gardener knew that digging around the base of the tree and adding manure to the soil was important, but he had done nothing until the vintner suggested that the tree be cut down. If they had both been better farmers, they wouldn't have waited. The story brings into question the judgment of the gardener and the vintner who hadn't properly nurtured this tree at the center of their vineyard.

Progressive church plants are called to be like fig trees in the vineyard. Surrounded by vines that all produce the same kind of fruit, we are asked to be something different. There may be varietals in the vineyard, but the fruit is always grapes. Our mission is to be different; we are to produce a different kind of fruit altogether. All Saints' hasn't gathered in Bentonville just to create a church like every other church in Benton County. We have a mandate to be something else. There is no owner who impatiently inspects the tree for fruit. As tenders of this tree in the vineyard, we are responsible for its care from the very beginning.

Throughout the country, churches like All Saints' are emerging from the endless trellises of sameness as fig trees that are rising up from the vineyard. These churches are set apart and at the same time uplift the whole. We aren't called to alienate those who believe they have found the truth, but to lift them up just as the branches of the fig tree lift the grapevines to new heights so that the grapes can produce the great vintage wine.

Shortly after one of the articles about the opening of All Saints' appeared in the local paper, the entire community caught wind of what we were doing. The article made a reference to something that I had said in an interview about the welcoming, inclusive nature of our community. Much to my surprise, a blogger in the community responded in a way I did not expect. Far from being hostile, this person asked his fellow Christians: "Why can't we do that? Why can't we be that generous, open, and accepting?" His message filled me with a hope that there will be a time when All Saints' does not stand alone in Bentonville in offering a message of unconditional acceptance to all God's children.

Most parables have a beginning, middle, and end. This one is different because it does not have an ending. The future of the fig tree is unresolved. Likewise, the future of All Saints' and other progressive church plants remains unresolved as well. What will our churches look like next year? What will our churches look like in the two or three years it takes for a sprout to be ready for planting? We just simply do not yet know. However, it is clear that the fate of the tree depends on those of us who tend to the young sapling. But it is also a lesson for us not to wait. We've just planted this tree; the time to nurture and care for its growth is not in a few years, but now when its roots are shallow and its branches are thin.

What sets All Saints' apart from the other churches in Bentonville is that we combine the ancient with the contemporary; we have a liturgy that is reminiscent of the early church and a theology that recognizes that we live in the age of reason. We welcome everyone. We regard scripture as divinely inspired, but not always to be taken literally. We are open-minded and we accept a degree of ambiguity. We aren't a church that is heavily into doctrine. One isn't required to accept a list of truths or submit to an outline of the faith in order to be accepted in our community. In our emerging church, doctrine isn't dogmatic, but is a practice of reflection and discussion and critique, then rethinking and rearticulating in the midst of an environment that is caring, loving, and considerate.

Brian McLaren writes, in his book *A Generous Orthodoxy,* "to be a Christian in a generously orthodox way is not to claim to have the truth captured, stuffed, and mounted on the wall. It is rather to be in a loving community of people who are seeking the truth on the road of mission and who have been launched on the quest by Jesus, who, with us, guides us still." Progressive church plants are called to be a different kind of church. We are called to bring a breath of fresh air into a stale church environment. We are called to offer something new, something emerging, and something changing. What will result from this sense of open-mindedness and our willingness to experiment remains to be seen. It is clear that we are not meant to be just another vine in the vineyard. Instead, we offer something old and something new. We offer the gospel expressed in a way that is truly good news. We offer the discovery that you can be Christian if you are unloved, questioning, uncertain, open-minded, political, and progressive. Together, may we spread our branches and grow our roots as fig trees in the vineyard.

Pentecost

"When the day of Pentecost had come, they were all together in one place. And suddenly from heaven there came a sound like the rush of a violent wind, and it filled the entire house where they were sitting. Divided tongues, as of fire, appeared among them, and a tongue rested on each of them. All of them were filled with the Holy Spirit and began to speak in other languages, as the Spirit gave them ability" (Acts 2:1–4).

If a typical resident of Benton County had fallen asleep, say, two decades ago, and awakened today and found themselves plopped down between the potatoes and the onions in the produce section of Walmart, they might accidently guess that it was the Day of Pentecost. This sleepy-eyed visitor to Walmart would be, like the witnesses to Pentecost described in Acts, "amazed and astonished" to find himself or herself in the midst of a diversity of class, culture, and language that we encounter every day in our unusual nook in the Ozarks.

If you have visited truly cosmopolitan cities like London, Paris, New York, Houston, Toronto, or Los Angeles you know that it is not surprising to encounter on the average street corner scenes that are reminiscent of the Day of Pentecost. People from "every nation under heaven," Jews, Cretans, and Arabs, residents from

Mesopotamia, Egypt, Libya, and Rome all collect together in the marketplace. We expect to find that kind of cultural richness in many large urban areas. But what your average demographer wouldn't expect to find, and why our freshly awakened time traveler in the produce section of the Bentonville Walmart would rub their eyes in amazement, is that this is a small town like no other. It is a small town where one can hear languages that are spoken in every corner of the planet. What an interesting development to take place in a part of the country where, well into the last century, there were more than a hundred "sundown towns," where people of color were graphically warned with a sign posted at the city limits: "Don't let the sun go down on you here."

Despite the recent changes, we have to admit that racism, mistrust, and fear of the "other" remain. I once had a conversation with a dear little lady in an assisted living facility. I love the "elders" as they are called in this home, partly because they are willing to honestly express sentiments that younger, more circumspect people are less willing to share with me. She had recently moved here from Little Rock to be near her children and because (and she paused here and looked me in the eye to see how I would react) "there were just getting to be too many different kinds of people." She obviously didn't get around much in Bentonville or she would have realized that she had jumped out of the frying pan and leaped into the fire. Indeed, the fire of Pentecost is a challenge that the world of Pentecost presents to us all.

Overall, the progression toward inclusiveness has been moving forward. Slavery was abolished. Women gained the right to vote. The civil rights movement and integration made racial discrimination more difficult. And I believe we can see a day when couples, regardless of their sexual orientation or gender identity and expression, can be fully accepted and their marriages recognized both by church and state. The question facing us now, is do we move forward along that path, or do we allow the impulsive, primitive fear of the outsider to prevent us from fully embracing the path of liberation, the spirit of Pentecost, that God has prepared for us?

Progressive church plants like All Saints' are on the frontier, the exciting edges of that evolution, and are uniquely called to embrace the very spirit of Pentecost. We can hang on to a fear of diversity that is still present in the larger community or we can stand with the original witnesses to Pentecost, "amazed and astonished." It takes courage to practice the hope of Pentecost in a world dominated by fear. On that day, the Holy Spirit moved among diverse cultures and religions in order to weave them together. At every Pentecost, we are reminded to stand together as a church to witness the in-breaking of the Holy Spirit. With the Holy Spirit, we are called to work to bring together all of humanity and to celebrate our differences, which ought to unite us in God's holy purpose.

Teacher, Let Me See

Not long after the community of All Saints' began celebrating Eucharist together at Washington Junior High School, I was very pleased when our young congregation could count among our already diverse group a faithful parishioner who was deaf. Her addition to the congregation added complexity and spiritual depth; her presence among us was a constant reminder that our perception of the love of God and our sense of the way God works in the world can be very different among different people. Later that year, the bishop's administrative assistant, Beth Matthews, sent out an e-mail to all the clergy in the Diocese of Arkansas, letting them know that a Book of Common Prayer printed in Braille had been donated to the diocese and was available to whoever might need it. Immediately, fearful that another priest might beat me to the punch, I quickly responded to the e-mail, explaining to Beth that we could use the prayer book, because we had a new parishioner who was deaf. After a short interval, during which she either collected her thoughts or perhaps circulated my e-mail around the diocesan office, Beth, in a kind and thoughtful voice that always comes across even in an e-mail, wrote, "Tell me, Roger, is your parishioner blind as well as deaf? If she isn't, I'm not sure that a Braille prayer book would be useful." She must have thought that it was the new vicar in Bentonville that had taken leave of his senses!

All Saints' began as a congregation that celebrated its diversity. We proclaim our welcoming nature on our website, on the masthead of our Sunday bulletin, and, I suspect, in response to anyone who asks, "What is All Saints' about, anyway?" We are rightly proud of the fact that sex, color, class, creed, sexual orientation, gender identity and expression, or ability present no barrier to inclusion in our midst. Yet sometimes I wonder if, in our eagerness to accept those whom other churches might not be so ready to welcome, we fail to notice that those who do the welcoming are the ones that stand the most to gain from the relationship. In welcoming the "other," we have the opportunity to see the world in ways to which we might have otherwise remained blind.

Our failure to fully embrace life is a kind of blindness, symptomatic of our inability to see the richness of God's providence. In Mark's Gospel, Jesus restored the sight of Bartimaeus, the blind man. But in truth, Bartimaeus could already see more clearly than his sighted neighbors. Bartimaeus, blind though he was, sensed the presence of the Holy when he heard the man Jesus pass him. Many in the crowd told Bartimaeus to be quiet, but instead Bartimaeus shouted, "Jesus, Son of David, have mercy on me."

In our diversity, we have the chance to call on the name of God in different voices and experience the presence of the Christ in a multitude of ways. We learn from those who are different from ourselves that the Divine cannot be limited by our narrow vision of God. May our prayer be that of Bartimaeus: "Teacher, let me see again."

Miracles

Some people come to All Saints' expecting miracles, while others come just hoping to be fed. And for many, finding a place where they can experience love and where they can find nourishment is a miracle beyond belief. This sort of miracle seemed to be in the making awhile back. It was one of those ordinary summer Sundays, another of the endless Sundays after Pentecost. Attendance was light, as it tends to be in the summer. The music was good, the sermon had gone as planned, and we were anticipating being nourished at the Eucharist.

However, the Holy Spirit, stealth-like as she often is, crept in at the end of the weekly announcements. I asked if there was anything else to bring to the attention of the congregation, when one of our parishioners stood from her place on the second row and handed me a note card. She asked that I read the card aloud. On the piece of paper was written a simple and eloquent message thanking the people of All Saints' for the love, concern, prayers, and food that she and her family had received after the unexpected death of her partner, the mother of the children that sat on either side of her. It was an unremarkable event in the life of All Saints', for it is just simply what we do as a church. The event, however, was made miraculous by the simple fact that there is probably not another church in Benton County where a partner in a same-sex relationship could so openly express her grief at the loss of her beloved. Indeed, the fact that we could be there for her and her family was a miracle.

Then, the door that allows the Holy Spirit into our midst was left ajar and another miracle occurred. I innocently asked if there were birthdays or anniversaries to celebrate that day. A new face in the crowd hesitantly raised her hand and said that it was her husband's birthday. Never being too sure about the exact nature of relationships at All Saints', I asked if the man beside her was the husband of whom she spoke. Unsmiling, she nodded yes. I asked him if he would like to come forward to receive a birthday blessing. He slowly and painfully rose from his seat, found his cane, and shuffled into the aisle. Seeing his difficulty, I said, "Wait, I'll come to you." But he held his hand up and said, "No, I can make it." I don't think that there was a single breath taken as the gathered congregation silently supported him on his staggering trip to the altar.

I asked for his name, he received our blessing, and then he returned to his seat. But perhaps the greatest miracle on that already miraculous morning occurred during coffee hour. As the couple sat side by side on a bench against the wall sipping coffee and eating quiche, dozens of parishioners came over to shake their hands and greet them. The couple spoke with pride, in the halting English of people who have difficulty with language, of their jobs in maintenance at Walmart Store One, just down the road in Rogers. They noted that because they are different, they are not often welcomed in churches. Ultimately, they were looking for a church that accepted them.

Their childlike smiles were wide as they assured me they would be back the following Sunday. To my happiness, they did come back and during the next few weeks, I received daily e-mails from both of them. They told me of the events of their simple lives, their plans, and their shared excitement over a future excursion to Eureka Springs. Then, and I can only surmise what happened, I suspect that they shared their joy at finding a welcoming church with a friend or coworker. And since the Episcopal Church is always in the news when we have a General Convention, their acquaintance must have told them that the church they were attending was part of a larger church that has gay priests and bishops and was also in the process of developing a rite for same-sex blessings.

It was not long before I received an e-mail from them written in rambling, parroted language about God's word, truth, and what is and what isn't considered to be an abomination. They concluded the e-mail by saying, "We are sorry Roger, but we will not be back." The e-mail broke my heart. Here was a couple who for years had searched for a community that would embrace them in all their imperfection. However, they live in a world so filled with prejudice and bigotry that they too were blinded to the realization that the love of Christ, a love that was extended to the disabled, to the imprisoned, to society's outcasts, the very love of Christ that was extended to them, is the same love that the church offers to our gay and lesbian brothers and sisters.

The church has the opportunity to extend the love of Christ to those that society rejects. It is the disabled, the immigrant, the person of color, the poor, and members of the gay and lesbian community that are most in need of Christ's love. It is the church's responsibility, as the body of Christ, to transmit that love to everyone. These miracle stories were important for the early church. In fact, the story of the feeding of the five thousand is the only miracle story included in all four Gospels. We need miracles too.

The miracle I would like to see would be every bit as fantastic as the transformation of the five loaves and two fishes to a feast sufficient for five thousand. It would be a miracle more gratifying than the sight of Jesus walking on water. The miracle I have in mind would be for the prejudice and bigotry, in all the ugly forms it takes, to fade away in every part of the world. My hope is for the church, rather than being the last to give up its prejudice against the outsider, to be the first to offer the way of Christ to others so that all God's children may be fed and experience the abundance of God's love. As Jesus told his disciples, "Gather up the fragments left over, so that nothing may be lost" (John 6:12). I pray, as Paul prayed in his letter to the Ephesians, "that you may have the power to comprehend, with all the saints, what is the breadth and length and height and depth, and to know the love of Christ that surpasses knowledge, so that you may be filled with all the fullness of God" (Eph 3:18–19).

Our Children

I've been thinking about the gift of children that we have at All Saints'. There is a growing abundance. Every Sunday, the entire gathered congregation gets to share in the delight and wonder that these children embody. Unfortunately, I know of Episcopal churches in the Diocese of Arkansas where there are no children at all. A few years ago a good friend, in the last months leading up to his death, told me that his favorite part of the worship service was the time when the kids return from Children's Chapel. He delighted in seeing these children search the crowd for their parents, proudly taking their place in the community. I can't tell you how many visitors have told me how much they enjoy hearing the voices of babies cooing and commenting during the service. They usually say, "You know, there are so many churches where if a baby cries out, people turn around and frown and make their disapproval known. Here at your church, people seem so comfortable with kids being kids."

They are right. Our children are among the things that make All Saints' a different kind of place. Lifting up children isn't just about tolerance for noise or even about how incredibly adorable children are, though they are so beautiful. I believe that the way a church regards children has much to do with the way Jesus regarded children. In Jesus's day, children were the ultimate symbol of powerlessness. Children were regarded as not quite persons, but as mere possessions of the father of the household. Jesus offered a very serious challenge to the social norms of the day when he took a child in his arms and proclaimed that when adults were welcoming children they were welcoming God into their midst.

One of the most vivid pictures I remember from my early childhood was depicted on the inside cover of the pale blue Bible I carried to Sunday school. It was a picture of Jesus looking down on a child he held in his arms. While it was a sweet portrayal, I think it missed the Gospel lesson. The point is not just that Jesus loves the little children, but that Jesus's love for the children is emblematic of his love for the downtrodden, the poor, and those who stand outside of the mainstream. Once again, we are confronted with the paradoxical nature of God's will and reign. Whoever welcomes one such child, the powerless among us, welcomes the Christ, himself.

Indeed, Jesus teaches us a different way. Just as he urges his disciples to put down their own striving for status and glory and to recognize that, in his kingdom the first will be last and the last will be first, he makes his point by holding a child before him, the ultimate symbol of powerlessness. True greatness requires that we bring our focus onto something other than ourselves. Greatness comes from welcoming one who is not considered great by the larger culture, those for whom the child is the exemplar, those beyond the inner circle, those who most need a welcome. When we welcome a child we welcome someone who does not possess accomplishments, status, or pretensions. Jesus asks us to welcome every person in the same way, without regard for external measures of their worldly importance, wealth, success, or failure.

To imitate children, as Jesus repeatedly asks us to do, provides us with an understanding of ourselves and helps us to realize that we are human beings loved by God. And we are loved not because of our own successes, honors, or accomplishments, as if what we had done might help us win favor with God, but in the sure and certain knowledge that we are loved just as a child is loved. As Jesus tells us, it is in being loved that we can experience the presence of his kingdom.

Forget the idea that this is one of those stories about the "nice Jesus" who is meek and mild. This is a story about who has power and who doesn't and it showcases Jesus's own desire to turn that world completely upside down. I often think about this gift of children at All Saints', and with their presence comes the great responsibility of caring for them, teaching them, and listening to them and their needs. Churches should listen to children because their presence is instructive, not just through the remarkable things they say and do, but because their presence serves to remind us of the vulnerable in our community, those who can't entirely care for themselves, those who are powerless and pushed aside, and those who still face discrimination. Jesus took the little child in his arms, not because it makes such a nice scene on stained glass, but because Jesus wanted to demonstrate to his disciples that everyone, but especially the lowly, are welcome into God's full embrace. As we welcome children, as we welcome the powerless, we welcome the Christ into our midst.

A Voice Crying in the Wilderness

In the fourth year of Barack Obama's presidency, when Mike Beebe was governor of Arkansas, Bob McCaslin was mayor of Bentonville, Greg Hines was mayor of Rogers, Frank Anderson was mayor of Bella Vista, Mike Duke was president and CEO of Walmart, and Rob Walton was chairman of the board of directors, the word of God came to the people of All Saints' in the wilderness. And they went into all the regions around the Ozarks, proclaiming a baptism of repentance for the forgiveness of sins, "...as it is written in the book of the words of the prophet Isaiah, The voice of one crying out in the wilderness . . ." (Luke 3:4).

When the author of Luke's Gospel chooses to call out the names and offices of seven historical, political, and powerful leaders, I think the evangelist does this not merely to set the tone for what he has to say, but to bring to our attention that the story he is about to tell, the story of the birth of Jesus, was grounded in real, substantive events, with real tension existing between the Roman and Jewish worlds, between the powerful and the powerless. We are to read the words of John the Baptizer, not as some far away fairy tale, but relevant to the reality of our existence, in this place, in the early twenty-first century.

What, in fact, would it look like if we answered the call, as John the Baptist did, to be a voice crying out in the wilderness? What would stop us from wrapping ourselves in the camel-skin cloak of John the Baptist, who dined on locusts and wild honey and proclaimed to all who would listen: "Prepare the way of the Lord"? Maybe what would stop us is the fact that we have grown too comfortable with the myths in which we choose to wrap ourselves instead.

A poem written by the Rev. Mark Sandlin begins like this:

> *Today, like the rest of the world,*
> *when I woke I wrapped myself in myths.*
> *They are comfortable and warming in what can seem*
> *   like such a cold world.*

*Yes, they are old and worn but they are familiar
and even the most fashion forward find comfort in this
thread-worn garb.*

John the Baptist came to dispel myths. We have myths of our own, such as "Love the sinner and hate the sin." I have quickly discovered that this phrase is used as a secret code by churches that pretend to welcome members of the LGBT community into their churches. Upon their arrival, they find that they are really only welcome if they change who they are or at least pretend to be straight.

"For you always have the poor with you" (Matt. 26:11). While Matthew's words lend credibility to this myth, the words can be easily twisted so that we excuse ourselves from doing anything to actually root out the causes of poverty, to seek justice on behalf of the poor, and do more than simply offer them charity. Consider another myth: "Everything happens for a reason." We wrap ourselves in this notion, imagining that God is responsible for allowing the most horrible atrocities such as untreated illness, violence, and neglect so that some unfathomable vision of God could play out. Mindlessly parroting such platitudes may make us feel more comfortable, but holding on to these myths is cold comfort for the victims of injustice and oppression. Not only is it bad theology, it is also evidence of our own unwillingness to put forth the effort to better understand the truth of how God works in the world. At a time when our leaders seem to lack the moral courage, conviction, and sense of vision to lead the people of our nation, it would serve us well to listen to the prophetic voice of John the Baptist, a voice unafraid to speak truth. The people are still stumbling in the dark, longing for light.

On Wednesday afternoons in the parish hall, usually around 4:00, well before the community meal is served at 5:30, a handful of hungry folks show up to get a good table, to get out of the weather, or maybe just to socialize for a little while. If I'm upstairs in my office, I can usually hear Doug's deep resonant voice rising above the chatter of his tablemates. I know that when I walk down the stairs he will be waiting for me. Doug is a big man, with large hands that reach out to grasp mine when I approach him. There is wildness about him reminiscent of John the Baptist, unkempt hair sometimes holding bits of leaves or grass, piercing eyes, and always wearing the same camouflaged hoodie. Looking as if he has just stepped out of the wilderness, he often shares his visions with me. For example, he tells a frequent tale of the demon that inhabits the space between the mattresses of his bed and who refuses to disappear permanently. So, I pray with him that the crooked shall be made straight and for the demons to depart and allow him to rest.

Doug is also troubled by his smoking habit. He knows he should quit and he does for a week or two, but his addiction gets the best of him and he just cannot resist. So, we pray that every valley will be filled, asking for God's mercy and strength. He also tells me of a coastal city in Florida that is waiting for him because they want to thank him for the relief work he did there after Hurricane Andrew. He believes that they have promised him a ticker tape parade in his honor and he wants to ride on a float and wave at the crowd. So, we pray that the rough ways will be made smooth so that he can find his way to Florida.

It has been made clear to me that Doug's voice is a voice crying, sobbing, and sometimes even wailing in the wilderness. Doug's voice is the voice of the poor, the troubled, and the abandoned who live in our midst. It is a voice that cries out, as clearly as the voice of John the Baptist, to "prepare the way of the Lord." It is a voice that won't let us forget that our country is ignoring the suffering around us. It is a voice offering us a baptism of repentance and forgiveness for the sins of a nation and a community that ignores the anguish of people like Doug who live in our communities.

Doug's presence offers us something more. When I pray with Doug that his demons be cast out from his mattresses, I'm also praying for release from the torment of my own demons. And when I ask on Doug's behalf for forgiveness for smoking another cigarette, I'm asking for forgiveness for my own transgressions. And when I listen to Doug's description of the ticker tape parade that awaits him on the Florida coast, I can't help but imagine a day when we will all come into the glory of God's presence.

A few weeks ago, I missed the Wednesday evening meal. When I walked into the office on Thursday, the church secretary said, "A big man named Doug left something for you yesterday." She pointed to the office table. Neatly folded atop the table was Doug's camouflaged hoodie. As I glanced at it on the table, she added: "He said you would like it." At first, I was a little confused. Then, I remembered that the week before I had admired his camo hoodie a little too much, noting how easy it would be for him to hide in the wilderness. So Doug, who owns almost nothing, literally gave me the coat off his back. Doug has a giving nature, but the camouflage hoodie, like the camel skin draped over John the Baptist's shoulders, was worn by one who's voice is crying out in the wilderness, crying out to a people who have grown more comfortable listening to myths, rather than to the truth. Like John the Baptist, Doug is a crazy prophet with a message worth listening to. To accept the message, to cast off the comfortable cloak of myth and don the Baptizer's camel skin, is to embrace John's message of repentance and to prepare the way of the Lord. In so doing, we prepare ourselves for the coming of the Messiah.

Jesus Said, "I Am the Gate for the Sheep"

We have a tendency to think of a gatekeeper as someone designated to restrict entry, perhaps a sentinel at the entrance to a military compound, a security guard at the entrance to a gated community, or even an administrative assistant who diligently protects access to the boss. All too often, churches have designated themselves as gate-keepers. They take on for themselves the role of determining who is admitted through the gate by requiring a set of beliefs or a particular course of action before someone can be accepted into the fold.

Let me present another possibility. Jesus said, "I am the gate." When you think of Jesus as the gate, imagine him with his arms wide open, gathering up all the differently colored sheep, the ones that are limping, those that are hungry, the sheep wearing a full wool coat and the ones that have already been shorn smooth and naked. In the verses that follow, Jesus says that he is the "good shepherd." This isn't a shepherd who is intent on culling the weak and the lame from his flock, nor a shepherd intent on maintaining the purity of his stock. Rather, this is a shepherd who welcomes every sheep who wanders by, every sheep who has learned that in this sheepfold all may have abundant life. This is the shepherd with his arms stretched wide open.

The church has, too often and for too long, presented an image of Jesus as the gate that is designed to keep people out. For too long, Christianity has heeded the voice of the thieves and bandits who divide and scatter the fold by insisting that the gate is narrow, that there is not room for all. The good shepherd brings in all the lost sheep without exception. The church's role is not to decide who gets in and who is left out of the sheepfold. If the church is the gatekeeper, then its job is to hold the gate wide open, making sure that God's abundant love is offered to everyone.

One day, I had lunch with a young couple from our parish with two very young children. They had been drawn to All Saints' for a variety of reasons, but partly because of the diversity that they had found in our congregation. During lunch we chatted amicably about family, work, and our building plans. Toward the end of our meal, the husband said, "I have something rather serious I'd like to bring up. We have a tremendous opportunity at All Saints' that doesn't exist elsewhere. I recognize that we are one church, with an English service and a Spanish service, but I want to make sure that we don't drift apart. I realize that there is something of a language barrier, but I think that we should do everything we can to overcome that barrier by planning activities that bring everyone together and promote unity."

As he and his wife spoke of their vision of All Saints', they imagined a church where their children worship, learn, and serve God among people of all races, nationalities, ages, sexual orientations, gender identities and expressions, political and theological leanings, and economic classes. They don't want their children raised in an atmosphere where they learn to merely tolerate difference and to love people who only look, act, and think like they do. Instead, they dream their kids will know people who don't have everything money can buy. They desire for their children to learn to not judge people by the color of their skin. They hope their children will know the richness that comes by exposure to different ways of being. Most importantly, they want their precious kids to avoid the fear and prejudice that emerges from ignorance of the unknown. Their vision is for All Saints' to be a church where diversity and inclusion abound. Put simply, their hope is for All Saints' to live into its name. In God's eyes, we are all saints.

We still live in a very segregated world. And it has been said that the most segregated place in America is church on Sunday morning. At All Saints', we have a very good start at moving against that trend. But I offer the following word of caution. There is a natural tendency for people to gravitate toward that which is familiar. For any progressive church plant to truly be one church, we have to embrace, nourish, and celebrate our diversity. We must issue a clarion call to the world around us declaring that we are one sheepfold and that the gate to the sheepfold remains wide open. Moreover, we must be very intentional about insuring that all within the sheepfold know that they are welcome.

To that end, All Saints' formed a taskforce to develop, foster, and promote activities that bring us into the company of one another. Our meeting place at Christ the King Church is too small to hold a combined bilingual service on Sundays, but we hold a bilingual service and parish picnic every year on the site where we will build. We plan bilingual events for the youth of All Saints'. A cooking school is planned, where cooks from El Salvador, Mexico, Guatemala, the Dominican Republic and every other Latin American country that is represented in the congregation introduce the distinctiveness of their cuisine to the rest of us. Bilingual services are also held throughout Advent, on Ash Wednesday, and during Holy Week. Creating and sustaining unity is an ongoing process that requires everyone to remain mindful of the fact that we are one church.

I once had the great pleasure of hearing the Dalai Lama speak in Fayetteville. His warmth, kindness, and sense of humor radiated throughout the audience. I have paraphrased a portion of his talk that speaks to the commitment to fostering unity in the midst of such great diversity: "My message is the practice of compassion, love, and kindness. Compassion can be put into practice if one recognizes the fact that every human being is a member of humanity and the human family regardless of differences in religion, culture, color, and creed. Deep down there is no difference." He reminded the crowd that "human beings are all the same; we all want happiness and need the opportunity to practice forgiveness." Indeed, this is the nature of the sheepfold we have gathered here at All Saints'. The church's task is to fling the gate wide open and to throw it off its hinges so that there is room for the entire sheepfold. And within that one sheepfold, may God provide us with ample opportunities to practice forgiveness and compassion and, in so doing, may we find a happiness that is lasting and fulfilling.

Belief

Diana Butler Bass's book *Christianity After Religion: The End of the Church and the Birth of a New Spiritual Awakening* is an exploration of the worldview of the increasing numbers of Americans who claim to be "spiritual, but not religious." Bass notes that this claim "is often a way of saying, 'I am dissatisfied with the way things are, and I want to find a new way of connecting with God, my neighbor, and my own life.'" Coinciding with a movement in society away from religion and toward spirituality, Bass imagines a shift from the "what" toward the "how." In other words, the issue of *what* a person believes becomes less important than *how* one believes or *how* a person puts their faith into practice.

Bass points out that our conception of the word "belief," as it is typically used in the New Testament, has hardened into a word denoting a firmly held opinion. The Latin that gave shape to contemporary theological thinking used the word *credo* to express what we now define as belief. When translated into English, *credo* actually comes closer to meaning, "I set my heart upon" or "I give my loyalty to." Our word "faith" really comes closer to expressing what was originally meant by belief. Bass goes on to suggest, "Indeed, in early English usage, you could not hold, claim, or possess a belief about God, but you could cherish, love, trust in, or devote yourself to God."

A picture of a much more inclusive kind of Christianity emerges if one holds a less doctrinal sense of the word "belief." Bass holds that instead of reading John 3:16 as "everyone who agrees that Jesus is the Son of God won't perish," it would be better read as, "everyone who directs his or her heart toward Jesus will not perish." This kind of interpretation presents to the reader a compelling invitation rather than a threat of condemnation. Furthermore, to believe in the resurrection in the "credo" sense has little to do with an agreement with the "facts" of the resurrection story as they are recounted in the scriptures. A rigid compliance with doctrinal truth seems to be far less meaningful to contemporary seekers of faith than trusting in an experience of resurrection that offers a real possibility for transformation in their own lives and in the lives of those they love.

The Cross: A Pathway to Compassion

I once heard the well-known New Testament scholar Amy-Jill Levine, professor of New Testament and Jewish studies at Vanderbilt Divinity School, speak on the presence of an unintentional anti-Jewish bias that pervades much of the preaching and teaching of the New Testament, particularly during Holy Week and Easter. A Jew herself, steeped in Torah, Talmud, and tradition, Dr. Levine was drawn to the story of Jesus when she was a child, attending Mass with her Roman Catholic friends almost as frequently as she attended synagogue. She regarded the church in her neighborhood as the other synagogue, simply the one her family hadn't joined. Her innocence regarding this interfaith arrangement continued until one of her playmates, no doubt repeating words she had learned at home, said to her: "You are a Jew, you killed Jesus."

These are words that were hurtful for a child to hear, but accusations of Jewish complicity in Jesus's death have been far more than hurtful for the generations of Jews throughout history that have suffered and died because of a misreading of scripture and a failure to grasp the Jewishness of Jesus, his disciples, and those he loved. Christians have been too ready to regard Jesus's claim that he came to fulfill the law as a rejection of the faith from which Christianity emerged.

Dr. Levine urges her Christian students to understand that it is not necessary to be critical of Judaism in order to proclaim what is good about Christianity. And neither is it necessary for Christians to condemn Muslims, Hindus, or Buddhists, in order to explain why our faith resides in Christ. There is no need to burn the Koran, scoff at Hindu religious practice, or criticize Buddhism in order to follow Christ. Instead, Dr. Levine compels us to ask ourselves the following question: "Why are we Christian? Why are we followers of Jesus?" We should resist taking the easy way out by answering that it is because we were born into a Christian home or into a Christian culture. Instead, we should ask the more challenging question: "What it is that draws us to choose the Christ?"

When reflecting on what it is that draws you to choose the Christ, it might be enough for you to simply accept Jesus's teachings in his Sermon on the Mount or hear who is blessed in the Beatitudes. I find that I'm compelled to follow the Christ because of the promise of the resurrection, not simply a hope for an afterlife but for the promise of a new life in this world. It is the possibility of resurrection that draws us to the Christ story. Life can be made whole and renewed; we can find God's presence in the now-ness of our existence. It is the gospel, the good news, which Christians have to proclaim. The resurrection is a particular manifestation of God's love for creation that is made explicit in the Christ story. However, Christians are often too ready to proclaim that the cross and the empty tomb are the symbols of an exclusive club, where belief in a narrowly held doctrine is the price of admission. Instead, we are called to embrace a more profound and inclusive understanding of Easter, as an eye-opening experience, revealing to us that a spark of divinity resides in all creation.

Imagine a resurrection that leads to a new life in which no one is regarded as the "other." The Easter season provides an opportunity for those of us who call ourselves Christ-followers to expand our circle of compassion. In fact, Christ's resurrection can be viewed as the perfection of his understanding of compassion. Of course, compassion for others was a central component of Jesus's teachings throughout his ministry, but it is the personal experience of suffering that truly enables one to understand the suffering of others and leads us toward compassion. And the cross, the Christian symbol of suffering and death, was the pathway that led to resurrection for the Christ.

Easter isn't simply a celebration of Christianity; it is also a commemoration of new life born of suffering on the cross. The way of the cross, therefore, becomes a gateway leading to compassion for all creatures, toward enlightenment, and to our resurrection as new beings. Our mission, as members of the dominant religion in the land, is to discover the compassionate spirit that lies at the heart of Easter and extend that same spirit to others in clear recognition that we are all one people and there is only one God.

CHAPTER 8

When You Open the Doors Wide, All Kinds of People Walk In

Do not neglect to show hospitality to strangers, for by doing that some have entertained angels without knowing it.

—Hebrews 13:2

Hospitality, the welcoming of the stranger, is firmly imbedded in the Christian tradition. If we look deeply at the source of hospitality we see how it is inextricably linked with Jesus's larger sense of social justice. Making a place at the table for the stranger is a way of saying, "I respect you, not because of who you are or the social position you occupy, but because you are a human being, one of God's children." Hospitality and justice go hand in hand. When hospitality is extended to all, regardless of wealth, status, color, sexual orientation, or gender identity and expression, God's justice is being done.

Hospitality isn't just a transaction; it is not a business deal, or a calculated gift with an anticipated return. It doesn't have anything to do with improving one's social status or enticing someone into some kind of commitment. Hospitality is an unconditional gesture, offered in love, with no obligations attached. If, as a church, our hospitality is intended for a particular kind of person at the exclusion of others, it is no longer authentic hospitality. The hospitality of Benedictine monasteries, the source of our own Anglican spirituality, is legendary. No one is ever turned away. However, we should not forget that hospitality is not just about an open door, but it is also about an open heart and an open mind.

Jesus's depiction of a wedding banquet is a foretaste of the banquet that is to come. If we are to be a people that take seriously the teachings of Jesus, then the place to practice this craft of authentic hospitality is surely his church. I like to think that we throw a party every Sunday. We hold a banquet here at the table and it's not our task to determine who gets a seat.

What we often consider to be moral actions are in reality acts of love and they are part of a larger Christian tradition of hospitality. Throughout our history, Christians addressed concerns about human dignity within their discussions and practices of hospitality. In relation to strangers, hospitality was a basic category for dealing with the importance of transcending social differences and breaking social boundaries that excluded certain kinds of persons. Hospitality is a way of recognizing the sacred worth of people who seem to have little to offer when assessed by worldly standards.

Coffee hour is important because it is a place where community is nurtured. It is also important because it is a place where we can welcome guests and make them feel at home. And hopefully, our guests will come back. We want them to return because we are an emerging church and we want to grow. But I think it serves a far more important purpose. This gathering after the Sunday morning Eucharist is sort of like the Eucharist itself; it is a place where God's justice must prevail. If the unidentified stranger isn't welcome to sit at the place of honor at our table, I think we are missing the point of Jesus's message.

At our coffee hour tables, justice and friendship become inseparable. Justice becomes, not an abstract notion, but an embodied idea. The need for justice and the need for love are both made flesh in the presence of the unknown guest. It is altogether possible that we are unwittingly entertaining the Christ who dwells in our midst.

The Guest Is Sacred

How might we think of the advice to "shake the dust off your feet" as a natural reaction to a failure to extend hospitality? In the ancient mideastern world, hospitality wasn't simply a question of practicing proper social graces. Offering hospitality to the traveler in the arid desert world was a matter of survival. As Roland de Vaux writes of the desert Bedouin people of Israel and Jordan, "Hospitality is a necessity of life in the desert, but among the nomads the necessity has become a virtue and a most highly esteemed one. The guest is sacred." In addition to providing food and shelter, the stranger that arrived at a home in this ancient world could also expect to have their dusty feet washed by the host or by a servant. If the disciples had dust to shake from their feet when leaving a house, it is strong evidence that they had not been properly welcomed; they had not been received hospitably. It's not just that their feet were dusty when they left, but they had also not been offered sustenance and they had not received the necessities of food and drink that they needed to survive in their desert surroundings.

For those among us who are different, those who stand out because of race, disability, sexual orientation, gender identity and expression, or because they believe that the Bible is too rich a resource for living to be reduced to a simple book of rules, or they are friends of the marginalized and the oppressed, or they, with the prophet Isaiah, wish to bring good news to the poor, or those others who enter through the doors of All Saints' seeking sanctuary, Benton County can be a desert.

All Saints' is here to provide an oasis in this desert. In this land, the scorching heat of prejudice, bigotry, and discrimination can sometimes beat down on those who do not conform to a particularly narrow conception of Christianity. Churches like All Saints' offer relief, sustenance, and the free-flowing waters of acceptance to all who are thirsty. Together, we offer the love of God to those who have not received it elsewhere. In the words of the Rev. Dr. Martin Luther King, "Love is the key that unlocks the door which leads to ultimate reality." May the love of God fling open our doors and mightily welcome the sacred guests who enter.

I Like to Dress Like a Lady

In the Gospel of Mark, it is written that Jesus, surrounded by a crowd, was alerted to the presence of his family. Jesus looks at the crowd of misfits and miscreants who are gathered around him and says, "Here are my mother and my brothers" (Mark 3:34). Ultimately, it is a lesson in family values. While the crowd tries to bring Jesus's attention to his biological kin, Jesus lets them know that his real family can be found among the tax collectors, sinners, unclean, poor, and all those others gathered around him because they couldn't find a welcoming place in proper society. It's the protectors of family values who get it wrong and fail to recognize who Jesus really is and what his mission is all about. Self-appointed protectors of family values are still active today as they try to define for others which relationships can be blessed and which cannot, thereby withholding the benefits of family from those in loving relationships that look different from their own.

At All Saints', we like to think of ourselves as a progressive, open-minded people who practice a distinct brand of radical hospitality. Occasionally, the Holy Spirit presents us with an opportunity to stretch our collective imagination, to expand the boundaries of family, and to push us beyond limited ideas of who is included in God's circle of love. One day, I received a phone call from a parishioner named Laura who works at the Samaritan Community Center. One of her clients, Gerald, who sometimes also volunteers at the center, had attracted her attention. Gerald explained to her that he had grown up in a church-going family and loved church, but had been unable to find a congregation in Benton County that would accept him. Gerald's limited social skills and his unconventional style of dress made him feel unwelcome in most houses of worship. I listened to Laura's story of Gerald's sweet spirit, his generous disposition, and his childlike innocence. Then she asked, "Do you think that Gerald could find a home at All Saints'?"

"I'm pretty confident of it," I replied.

I gave Gerald a call and we arranged to meet. He wore carefully pressed slacks and a clean, collared shirt. His face was freshly shaven. His slightly curly hair was neatly parted in the middle and lightly brushed the top of his shoulders when he turned his head. The only thing unusual that I noticed about his appearance was the slight hint of mascara that I thought might have been around his twinkling eyes. In halting speech, each syllable slowly enunciated, in a kind of staccato-like pacing, Gerald began to tell me his story. "I have Asperger's Syndrome. I've looked it up. I've read about it. Do you know what that is?" I assured him that I did.

"I know a lot of things," he assured me. "I read a lot." Gerald then began describing in exquisite detail how, on his mother's side of his family, there were eight generations of clergy. After hearing him demonstrate his command of three disparate subject areas, and before he could start another, I interrupted him.

"Gerald," I said, "I'm pretty sure you would be welcome at All Saints'. We are a rather hospitable group."

"Well," he said, "I've been told that before, but then people try to change me. You see," he timidly offered, "I like to dress like a lady."

"Yeah, I've heard," I said, "Laura told me."

At that point, Gerald began to tell me of his childhood and of his desire, since he was old enough to choose clothes, to put on his sister's dresses. "It's part of who I am. I can't really explain it. It's just who I am," he said.

"Gerald, I wouldn't worry about it too much," I said. "A lot of us wear dresses here. When the priests and deacons at All Saints' arrive at church on Sunday, they go upstairs to the sacristy wearing pants and come down the stairs wearing long flowing white gowns. I think you will feel right at home here." And I am delighted to report that he has. Most Sundays you can find Gerald (or Geraldine, as she prefers to be addressed when dressed "like a lady") colorfully attired in the clothing that suits her, proudly occupying a pew in the midst of the people of All Saints'.

There are certainly those in the larger community, and possibly within our own congregation, who would say, "Roger, you have really gone too far now. You have now pushed the boundaries of God's love beyond where I can comfortably go." But I've come to recognize that uncomfortable sensation as the prickly presence of the Holy Spirit, who pushes me to a place beyond where I really want to go and redefines for me my understanding of family.

In the months and years since our initial meeting, Geraldine has grown comfortable enough as a member of our family to freely dispense advice on fashion, makeup, and deportment. In fact, if finishing schools for girls were still in vogue, Geraldine could have joined the faculty. She exhibits a singular devotion to achieving proficiency at any undertaking that interests her. Applying makeup clearly interests her. She explains the process: "Before I come to church on Sunday I always shave as closely as I can. Then I put on some foundation. Do you know what foundation is? Then concealer under my eyes and some powder, 'cause I don't want my face to be too shiny. Then some shadow on my eyelids. I like to curl my eyelashes, but that's hard 'cause they aren't very long. Then I brush on mascara. And sometimes I brush a little blush on my cheeks."

As Geraldine offered this tutorial to two teenage girls, their jaws were agape, their eyes wide, but they clearly listened to her advice. I suspect they secretly absorbed the lesson for future use. Sitting in church next to my wife, Cindee, Geraldine noticed that Cindee had crossed her long legs as she listened to the sermon. Geraldine began to fidget and cast a sideways glance in Cindee's direction. In the pause between the sermon and the recitation of the Nicene Creed, Geraldine leaned over to Cindee and said, "It's more lady-like to cross your legs at your ankles, besides you're less likely to get varicose veins."

CHAPTER 9

School of Love, College of Justice

We know love by this, that he laid down his life for us—and we ought to lay down our lives for one another. How does God's love abide in anyone who has the world's goods and sees a brother or sister in need and yet refuses help? Little children, let us love, not in word or speech, but in truth and action.

—1 John 3:16–18

When it comes to planting a church, I am less concerned about the bricks that are used to construct an actual building and more interested in mixing the mortar that binds a church together in Christian fellowship. Planting a church is really about the process of creating friendship, or "spiritual friend-ship," as the twelfth-century writer St. Abbot Aelred believed.

The funny thing is that we don't get to choose our friends. When I look around the table at the people who have newly gath-ered in one of our small groups, I am amazed that such a disparate collection of folks can be seated at one table. Age, income, ethnicity, sexual orientation, gender identity and expression, and religious background vary greatly. They seem to have little in common with each other except, perhaps, an openness, a receptivity, and a desire to explore a new spiritual path in community with others. These are not people who would normally be friends; when you choose to be a friend of Jesus, you don't get to choose your friends.

It is a natural thing to be drawn to those who are like us. We are put together, biologically, in a way that causes us to love our fami-lies. According to the principles of evolutionary theory, the quali-ties of love and nurturing are naturally selected for. More of our own genes will make it into the gene pool if we protect, care for, and love our progeny. By extension, we need the support of family members to ensure that our own offspring survive and flourish. It is fairly easy to love our families. Even beyond our families, a case can be made that we are biologically conditioned to create relationships with those who are similar to us. It is an easy thing to love those who share our values, our experiences, and who look like we do.

However, that's not what we, as Christians, are called to do. We are called to do something much more difficult. We are called to love those who are not like us. If we are serious about the Christian faith, we no longer get to choose our friends. The example of Christ is one in which he reached out to the margins of society, to the for-eigner, the poor, the sinner, and those shunned by the establish-ment. He sought his friends among the unlovable. As Christians, we are asked to do the same. As we just heard in the Gospel of John, "You did not choose me, but I chose you." And just as we did not choose to be loved by Christ, we cannot choose to exclude others from the love of Christ. Our commandment is to love one another, as Christ loved us.

The central role played by the church is a working out of our salvation in and through community. When we think of the church as the body of Christ, we rediscover that the gospel is also incarnational. Jesus Christ represents the historical fleshing out of God's love for humanity. What God wants to do is duplicate that once-in-history manifestation of his love throughout all history by putting the same life that was in his Son into groups of people learning to love one another and teaching their children to do the same. This is church. Welcome to the school of love.

They Will Know Us by Our Love

In the Book of Revelation, we read how "the one who was seated on the throne" says, "See, I am making all things new." Seeing all things new is part of the great joy of a church plant. Every Sunday ought to feel like springtime. There is no telling what plant will begin to bud or what idea will soon hatch. But then there is this pesky business of the new commandment: love one another. Wouldn't it be easier if we just forged ahead and planned new services, classes, and programs to increase community involvement? But if we did that, how would they know us? Would they know we are Christians because we built the most magnificent building in Benton County? Would they know that we were disciples of Jesus because we erected three giant concrete crosses alongside the freeway? Or will they know us because we love one another? Carlos Valles believes, "If you always imagine God in the same way, no matter how true and beautiful it may be, you will not be able to receive the gift of the new ways he has ready for you."

Before traveling to New York City one week, I needed to wash a few clothes. At the neighborhood laundromat, a place I typically avoid until I have absolutely nothing left to wear, I discovered that the change machine wouldn't accept my last crumpled dollar bill. I walked next door to the rundown mechanic's shop and framed my request in a way meant to elicit a favorable response. I said, "Being next door to a laundromat, I bet you guys get bugged all the time for change." And sheepishly holding up my crumpled dollar bill, I asked, "But do you have four quarters?" The guy behind the counter opened the cash register and announced that he had three, while the grease covered mechanic leaning against the door frame said, "I think I've got one." At the same time, I noticed that a customer was digging around in his pockets, eager to comply with my request.

I thanked all three of them and returned to the laundromat, put my wet jeans in the dryer, and dropped the freely given quarters into the slot. Seeking sanctuary from the heat, noise, and grime of the shabby laundromat, not to mention the overbearing gaze of Dr. Phil beaming down at me from the television perched above the fray, I went to my truck parked out front. Twenty minutes later, after I had become irrationally absorbed in the two-year-old issue of *Good Housekeeping* I had picked up inside, I noticed a woman standing at the front door. When I raised my head, she pointed in the direction of the bank of driers and said, "Sir, your dryer has stopped." I nodded my thanks. As I folded my clothes on the worn Formica table, I thought of the city I was preparing to visit. In New York City, it is not absolutely imperative that the customer always be proven wrong. However I've noticed that it is at least necessary that the customer always be made to feel that they are wrong.

I have found the people of Northwest Arkansas to be over-whelmingly friendly and hospitable. The South has always been known for its cordiality, but Christians aren't just called to be nice. Jesus didn't say, "Just as I have been friendly to you, you also should be friendly toward one another. By this everyone will know that you are my disciples, if you are friendly." From its inception, the people of All Saints' have known that they have been called to love and to offer a place that includes all God's children. But the kind of love to which Jesus called his disciples isn't an airy-fairy sort of love, but rather it's a boots-on-the-ground kind of love.

Being called to love might mean a change of identity and it might mean becoming something new, living in new ways, and worshiping in new ways. Being called to love might require change.

Church plants must keep the following question at the forefront: How are they going to know us? If we are to be the kind of disciples that Jesus has asked us to be, "They will know us by our love."

Twisted Vines

I'm not sure that Jesus had the church in mind when he told the parable of the vine and the vine grower, but I wouldn't be the first to notice that there are parallels between the vine and the church. In fact, the image of the vine with its twisting and growing branches feels a lot like All Saints'. As the community grows, our lives become increasingly intertwined. Our pains and joys cross and touch each other and opportunities to exhibit grace, practice forgiveness, and demonstrate love become more frequent. As the vines spread and we grow in faith, our roots dig deeper, searching for meaning and for sustenance. And we all bring to this vineyard a dung heap of lost love and broken dreams. But that is the stuff that brings substance and fertility to the soil on which this church and others are planted. Manure makes for very fertile ground. And it is from that rich manure-filled soil that new life emerges. New, green, vibrant branches will form and old branches, old tired ways of being, will fall away. And we as a people, sharing the love of God, will learn to love one another.

"All you really have to do is learn to love the people," was the advice my seminary professor, Charlie Cook, offered me and my fellow seminarians for succeeding in parish work. "You can get by with saying most anything from the pulpit, if you love the people." It turns out that he is right. The problem is, the people aren't always so lovable. How can I obey a command to practice love? This is what Jesus asked of his disciples, that they love as he loved them. He demonstrated for them a path of compassion and on the cross he showed just how far he was willing to go to sacrifice for them. Instead of a commandment to love, consider Jesus's advice to his disciples translated in this way: "I have loved you in order that you also love one another." It is not so much that it is a new commandment, but that the example of Christ can enable and empower us to love in a new way.

In the not-too-distant future, the All Saints' congregation will worship together in a permanent, beautiful sacred space at the north end of Main Street. In the midst of architectural splendor, it is likely that a sense of the transcendent will be more readily accessible. As our acolytes grow older and experienced, it is likely that they will carry themselves with more dignity and grace. Our music grows more beautiful each Sunday, as hymns grow familiar and as our choir grows in number and skill. A new building and an enhanced worship experience will likely mean that even greater numbers of visitors will find their way to All Saints'. Ultimately, the future of All Saints' will be determined, not so much by the music, or the architecture, or the quality of the sermons, but by how successful its members are at demonstrating their love for each other. As Jesus said, "By this everyone will know that you are my disciples, if you have love for one another" (John 13:35). If we follow that advice, every visitor who enters our holy space will know that they are in the midst of Christ's disciples.

Empathy

I heard a report on NPR about a study with lab mice in which the presence of empathy was explored. Injecting mice with a drug that caused mild stomach pain caused the mice to writhe in pain. Other mice present did not writhe in empathy except in the case of those mice that had shared a cage for a few weeks. These mice writhed in empathy when a mouse from their same cage had been injected with the stomach-pain-inducing drug. Human beings are capable of great empathy. Perhaps because of the long period it takes for our young to reach adulthood, it is imperative for the survival of our species that we care for our young and those in our kinship group. We are naturally drawn to empathize with those like us. But, as Christians, we are called to do much more. Loving those like us comes naturally, while loving those who are different doesn't. But that is precisely the example of Christ, who loved the Gentiles, lepers, sinners, women without stature, and poor. He reached out to people who were different from him. It's no wonder that it shocked the world or even that it got him executed. It's not a popular notion anywhere because it is so countercultural. But that is exactly what we are called to do as Christians. We are called to love people who are not like us.

Jesus, They Have No Wine

From the darkest days of World War II and for seventy years thereafter until January 2013, a thirsty out-of-town customer wandering up and down the aisles of any Benton County retail grocer might have echoed the words of the mother of Jesus at the wedding at Cana of Galilee, "They have no wine." This has now since changed and the proprietors of fifty or so E-Z Marts, Kum & Go's, and Walmarts are rejoicing, while teetotaling Baptists are, rather quietly I've noticed, gnashing their teeth. Only a few years earlier, the legal sale of beer and wine in Benton County would have required a turn of events no less miraculous than Jesus's conversion of plain water into fine wine.

Of course, it had already been remarkably easy to get an ice cold Bud or a sparkling chardonnay at dozens, perhaps even hundreds, of restaurants in Benton County. Membership in these "private clubs" may require that you add your name to a list, or perhaps only walk through the front door. Have you thought about why this change in attitude toward alcohol sales has come about so quickly? Certainly, the change in laws would not have happened without the support of those with the wherewithal to promote and implement the change. But at its heart, I think that a sea change of this sort is a reflection of an atmosphere of abundance that pervades Bentonville and the surrounding area.

Were it not for the wealth, and the opportunity for the creation of wealth, in this community, people from all corners of the globe would have not been drawn here. A life of abundance, as evidenced by the presence of fine restaurants, a vibrant downtown, bike trails, dog parks, a world-class art museum, and multiple employment opportunities have brought all kinds of people to Bentonville. These are common people who think it's rather nice to have a glass of wine with dinner and who are willing to sign a petition to help make that possible.

You don't have to look very far to see that the abundance isn't very evenly distributed. If you show up at any local food pantry, you will find people who are hungry. These are people who experience hunger in the midst of plenty. The enormous disparity in wealth, the growing gap between the rich and the poor, isn't something that we imagine taking place in lands far away; it is oftentimes right where we live.

The abundant life that God wants for all people, a life symbolized by a wedding banquet with stone jars filled to the brim with good wine, is not known by these hungry families. The sparseness of their existence ought to compel us, like the mother of Jesus, to tap on Jesus's shoulder, to point to those without food, shelter, and health care and to say, "Jesus, they have no wine." These families should also be the recipients of the promise of abundance that is voiced by the prophet Isaiah:

> How priceless is your love, O God!
> Your people take refuge under the shadow of your wings.
> They feast upon the abundance of your house;
> You give them drink from the river of your delights.
> (Psalm 36:7–8)

For many, the promise that they will drink from the river of God's delightful abundance remains a promise that is unfulfilled. The conversation between Jesus and his mother at the Wedding of Cana reminds me of the relationship between the Rev. Dr. Martin Luther King, Jr. and Rosa Parks, the extraordinary woman who in 1955 courageously refused to no longer accept the humiliation of giving up her seat to a white person on a bus in Montgomery,

Alabama. It was the subsequent arrest of Parks that prompted King to call for a boycott of the buses in Montgomery. Until that moment in history, King was not certain that the time had come for the civil rights movement to move forward. It was the action of Parks, tugging at King's sleeve, that told him: "There is no wine." This was the catalyst for extraordinary change in American history.

It's not that God doesn't want us to enjoy the fine wine. Apparently, Jesus, along with his disciples, was ready for a party. And judging from the quantity of fine wine that arrived, six stone jars holding twenty or thirty gallons each, we can imagine that they were in for quite a party. We are meant to enjoy the good life, but we forget that Jesus's invitation was for everyone to join the party. The good wine is for everyone, not just a select and privileged few.

After alerting Jesus to the absence of wine, his mother said to the servants: "Do whatever he tells you." In John's Gospel, this miracle at the Wedding of Cana marks the beginning of Jesus's ministry. Through Jesus's words and his actions, he explained to his disciples and to the world exactly what it is we are called to do. It is in the process of inviting everyone to the party that we also invite the prospect for personal transformation. Jesus's miracle of turning the water into wine is emblematic of the miracle that can take place in our own lives as well. Truly, a watery, self-interested kind of existence can be transformed into something resembling a rich, full-bodied cabernet.

Possessed by Demons

I was asked to come to an apartment at Havenwood, the women's transitional housing facility, to bless the rooms that have been painted and repaired for a new resident. Presiding at the celebration for a new home, asking for the grace of God's presence, that the inhabitants may know God, and that God would defend the household, is one of the great pleasures of my job. On such an occasion, family and friends collect at the doorway of the house and ask that God watch over the comings and goings of those passing through the threshold. Then, we process from one room to another, sprinkling holy water, usually with a rosemary branch, into the air and often onto the occupants of each room, all the while asking for God's blessing on the cooking in the kitchen, the slumber in the bedroom, learning in the study, and cleansing in the bath.

In the case of the apartment at Havenwood, those who were gathered celebrated the restoration of a new home. I also sensed that, contained within the desire for celebration, was also a feeling of needing to cast out any unclean spirits that might still linger behind the freshly painted walls. Almost certainly, the scarred walls of the apartment heard voices rise in anger, the tattered furniture had felt the heavy weight of bodies collapsing with exhaust, and the worn tile floors have received tears cried in anguish.

On the day the dwelling is blessed, in a setting that has known violence and despair, I offer the following invocation: "Let the mighty power of the Holy God be present in this place to banish from it every unclean spirit, to cleanse it from every residue of evil, to make it a secure habitation for those who dwell in it; in the Name of Jesus Christ our Lord. Amen." These are powerful words, but I have no more authority to drive out evil than any other person. We all have the capacity to invoke God's presence. Those who painted the walls, laid the floors, and who will donate the furnishings have, in their actions, called forth God's blessing.

The need for expelling any unclean spirits isn't limited to an apartment that has been possessed by the spirit of violence, heartache, and misery. Who among us hasn't known what it feels like to be possessed? Who hasn't been possessed by anger at a colleague or a family member? Who hasn't been possessed by jealousy? And who is not, from time to time, possessed by anxiety, greed, insecurity, or fear?

Jesus walks into our world of troubling possessions. The Christ speaks with authority and silences the voices within us that tell us we aren't good enough, smart enough, or strong enough. Jesus underscores his teaching in the synagogue with a demonstration of his power to silence the voices of the demons within us as well.

Distracted by the Poor

Gary, the first deacon to serve our congregation, returned home one day troubled and frustrated from a meeting of area clergy that administer a fund on which the social service agency where he works depends. Perhaps imagining that churches in Northwest Arkansas had something in common with circumstances facing the early church leadership described in Acts, one of the pastors proclaimed, "I go back to the early church. The devil tried to stop them every way he could. First, he tried persecution, but that only scattered them out further. Then he tried deceit and quoted the Ananias passages. That did not work either, so he tried the most powerful tool of all and that is 'distraction.' The people of the early church complained that their widows were not being taken care of. But the Apostles saw through the plot and assigned men to go deal with the problem. And the disciples said, '. . . while we for our part, will devote ourselves to prayer and serving the Word.' We must be careful not to become distracted by the poor."

The good pastor's concern with being "distracted by the poor" calls into question the very nature of ministry. While the New Testament has a handful of words that can be translated as ministry, the word *diakonia*, from which we get the English word "deacon," is ubiquitous. In its purest form, the work of the diakonia is that of serving, literally, "waiting on tables." In the Episcopal Church, the role is specifically assigned to an order of ordained clergy, but in reality, all Christians are called to this work. The qualifications for the job, as outlined in Acts, are that the servers of bread be "of good standing, full of the Spirit and wisdom" (Acts 6:3).

Rather than being distracted by the poor, it is our work with them that enables us to see with clear vision the true mission of the church. It is the poor that point us toward the Christ. Too often, we act as if our charitable work is done solely to feed the bellies and clothe the bodies of the needy. In reality, it is the giver that is transformed by the act of giving.

A narrow conception of what is meant by salvation and an overarching concern with enabling sinners to avoid the "fires of damnation" is too often the distraction that takes a Christian's mind away from the work that Jesus repeatedly calls us to do on earth. The blessing we are promised flows naturally from our engagement in the work of promoting God's kingdom. Matthew's Gospel relates Jesus's message, "For I was hungry and you gave me something to eat, I was thirsty and you gave me something to drink, I was a stranger and you welcomed me, I needed clothes and you clothed me, I was sick and you looked after me, I was in prison and you visited me" (Matt. 25:35–36). The poor and the Christ are one. In the eyes of the poor we are granted a glimpse of the Divine. Far from being a distraction, the poor are our blessing and the means of our salvation.

A Minimum Wage

Dom Helder Camara, the archbishop of São Paulo, famously said, "When I fed the poor, they called me a saint. When I asked why are the poor hungry, they called me a communist." As I watch the crowds of people who gather early at the All Saints' and Christ the King food pantry every Wednesday afternoon, I increasingly ask myself why so many people cannot afford to feed their families. We church people take pride in gathering and distributing food to the needy, but seldom ask why, in a land of such plenty, hunger exists at all.

Of course, the causes of poverty are multifaceted. Disability, either physical or mental, prevents some people from working. And others, even as unemployment rates have fallen in Northwest Arkansas, still can't find work. But I've noticed that growing numbers of people who come to the church seeking assistance are employed, or come from families where the principle breadwinner is working multiple jobs, but is paid a wage that keeps the family poor. It is apparent that low wages are keeping many hard working people mired in poverty.

I heard philanthropist and Microsoft founder, Bill Gates, once asked by a morning news interviewer what he thought about raising the minimum wage. He raised common objections about how increasing the minimum wage might lead to mechanization of the low wage earners job, or how raising the wage in one "jurisdiction" might lead employers to move elsewhere, or whether teenagers from wealthy households constitute the bulk of minimum wage earners.

A few minutes later that morning, mulling over Mr. Gates's comments in my mind, I stopped at McDonald's to buy an egg biscuit for breakfast. As the middle-aged woman behind the counter at McDonald's handed me a steaming cup of coffee, I asked, "How would it affect you if the minimum wage was raised to $10 an hour?" With tired eyes, she looked up from the cash register and replied, "It would change my life. I'm a single mom. It's impossible to make ends meet. It would change my life."

I looked around the restaurant kitchen and at the drive-through window for the teenaged sons and daughters of the wealthy that Bill Gates had referenced, but instead saw four other women, one in her sixties, the others maybe in their mid-forties. "Does everyone here make minimum wage?" I asked. "Close to it," she replied. Suddenly, I found myself surrounded by these women, each excitedly telling me how they worked multiple jobs that, on a good week, paid them $300. From their meager check they had to pay rent, utilities, a car payment, and provide food and clothes for their children. They quickly calculated that instead of $300 a week, raising the minimum wage to $10 an hours would mean that they could make $400 a week. "For me, that would make all the difference in the world," one woman sighed, while the others nodded in agreement.

I'm not sure if it was because I wore a clerical collar and they recognized me as a priest, or if I was the only customer who had ever inquired about their economic well-being, but one of the women, using a McDonald's napkin to wipe away a tear, looked up at me and asked, "Can you do anything about this?" Simply by asking the question, I had raised their expectations. And the earnest looks on their faces convinced me that I could not simply offer them false hope. "I don't know," I said, "but I'll do what I can."

So here is my proposal. I have little confidence that a gridlocked Congress will raise the federal minimum wage. Legislation at the state level appears unlikely to pass. Bentonville is the most prosperous city in the state and it is almost impossible for a minimum wage earner to live here. Let's change what we can, here and now. If you are a Bentonville employer, pledge to pay no one less than $10 an hour. If you live in Bentonville, ask your city council representative to support a local ordinance to raise the minimum wage. Finally, if you are unwilling to do either of those things, then just listen to the stories of the working poor.

It is difficult for those of us who are wealthy to really understand what it is like to work hard and still live in poverty. The next time a fast food worker hands you a McMuffin or a cashier hands you your change, ask what it's like to live on minimum wage. Their answer might change your life and, if you are willing to respond, you just might change theirs as well.

Charity and Justice

Here is how the prophet Isaiah described the mandate he received from God: "to bring good news to the oppressed, to bind up the broken-hearted, to proclaim liberty to the captives, and release to the prisoners; to proclaim the year of the LORD's favor" (Isa. 61:1–2). Jesus was quite explicit in his directive to feed the hungry, welcome the stranger, visit the imprisoned, care for the sick, and clothe the needy. In response to the frequent scriptural admonitions to reach out to the marginalized, many churches have become quite good at addressing the immediate needs of the sick, poor, and homeless that they encounter. And they should. Without the charitable acts of churches, many more people would go hungry, unclothed, and ill-housed. However, as followers in the Abrahamic tradition, we seem to have largely ignored the fact that we are called to engage, not only in charitable acts, but to work for justice on behalf of the marginalized as well. We behave as if we are only called to treat the symptoms of the illnesses that afflict society and to ignore the underlying disease.

It is good to sit at the bedside of the sick, but when adequate health care is unavailable for all, justice does not prevail. We are performing laudable acts of service when we open our food pantries to the hungry, but when working long hours for minimum wage still leaves families in poverty, justice is not done. We may extend a welcoming hand to the families that visit our churches, but when we fail to provide a path to citizenship for the immigrant seeking a better life in our midst, we have not truly welcomed the stranger. We may hold classes on marriage enrichment, but when we fail to provide a legal way for same-sex couples to demonstrate their commitment and fidelity to one another, we fail to bind up the brokenhearted and justice is not served. And we might start a prison ministry, but when we are so quick to incarcerate our children, and allow the jailer to feed prisoners only cold food, justice is denied.

It is mandated by scripture that we engage in acts of charity. However, it is good to recognize that, while the recipients of charity may benefit from the act, the ultimate beneficiary is the giver. Charity soothes the soul of the giver and allows us to feel that we are doing good in the world. Charity also allows the giver to remain in control. The benefactor determines to whom and under what conditions goods and services are allocated to the needy. Justice requires a letting go of control and an empowerment of others to act on their own behalf. And the result of granting power to the powerless may not be exactly what the giver had in mind.

Ultimately justice and charity must work in tandem, hand in hand. Charity soothes consciences and hungry stomachs may be filled. But transformation of the heart and soul, the ultimate work of God in the world, takes place through a change in the nature of all our relationships, and justice lies at the heart of that change. When we are brought into a just relationship with others, one that breaks down the artificial barriers between the powerful and the powerless, we begin to walk on ground where true transformation can take place.

CHAPTER 10

Welcoming the Stranger

The alien who resides with you shall be to you as the citizen among you; you shall love the alien as yourself, for you were aliens in the land of Egypt: I am the LORD your God.

—Leviticus 19:34

In February 2008, All Saints' received official status as an "organized mission" of the Episcopal Church of the United States, the newest mission in the Diocese of Arkansas. It all sounded very official; I even feared it sounded a little Pharisaic. I was grateful for the recognition of the work we had done in establishing this body of Christ. But it's that word "establishment" that made me squirm a bit, knowing that from the beginning it has been part of the ethos of All Saints' to allow the Spirit to blow where she will. And I pray that nothing we establish will ever prevent us from being born of the Spirit.

So what did it mean for us as a community to be born anew when we left the delivery room only one short year earlier? The challenge was to retain an openness to the continued movement of God's spirit in our midst in new and unexpected ways and to always guard against the tendency to say as a church: "This is the way we've always done it."

One of the best things about my job is that I get to say, "Yes." There is nothing I like better than when a member of All Saints' comes to me and says, "I would like to do this, what do you think?" And I have the pleasure of responding to his or her request with "Yes! Let's do that." This is typical of the way the Spirit moves among our people. I also get to say "yes" to myself. As a church planter, I frequently get ideas about how we might go about sharing a gospel of love and inclusion in Northwest Arkansas. Some ideas seem outright brilliant at the moment of conception but turn out to be flat stupid, while others that seem harebrained at first manage to bear fruit.

The Spanish translation of All Saints' is *Todos Los Santos*. The ESL classes that we offer are growing. Shortly after they first started, I was becoming discouraged about the low attendance. Thinking about where I might find Benton County's largest concentration of non-English speakers, I thought it would be a fine idea to distribute the fliers advertising the ESL classes at *una tienda* (a small grocery store). And then an even better idea came to me: to pass the fliers out during a change of shift at the local poultry processing plants. A beautiful thing about my job is that when I get an idea I'm often able to act on it immediately. So I gathered the fliers and made my way to Ozark Mountain Poultry on West Easy Street in Rogers. I passed out a few fliers in the parking lot as I made my way toward a very large white, boxy building. I thought I was at the main entrance, but after a Spanish-speaking woman used her plastic entry card to unlock the door for me, I realized that I had unintentionally made my way into the building through the employee's entrance.

"*¿Donde esta la oficina?*" I asked her. Her directions to the office were long and complicated, but I followed them as best I could. I made my way down twisting corridors, through employee changing rooms, and eventually found myself inside a very large dining hall. The windowless walls, the floor, and the plastic tables were as dazzling white as Jesus's garments at the Transfiguration. Neatly arrayed atop row after row of dining hall tables was an endless procession of lunch boxes of every color you can imagine, each containing the tacos and tortas that would sustain the workers through the long shift at the plant.

Again, I asked, "*¿Donde esta la oficina?*" And again, I was directed through *una puerta,* a door, and down a corridor. At the end of a cold cavernous hallway I could see a wide portal, but a curtain of translucent plastic ribbons hanging from the header above obscured the view inside. Suddenly, as I stood at the doorway, a breeze parted the curtain and I crossed the threshold into the heart of the processing plant. Unlike the lunchroom where the stark whiteness was punctuated by the vivid color of the waiting lunchboxes, the whiteness there was complete. Florescent lights looming high above the factory floor bleached the room of all shadows. Five hundred human figures, arrayed in white from head to toe, paper hats and surgical masks obscuring all but their eyes, standing at row after row of conveyor belts laden with the bodies of dead birds, suddenly and for a moment, ceased their labor and a thousand eyes, dark and penetrating, fell on me. I smiled and nodded and the thousand dark eyes smiled back at me. I was born anew.

Returning the Favor

I once lived on a short street in a barrio called Boyle Heights in East Los Angeles. Fifty years ago, this was a Jewish neighborhood, an immigrant population with Jewish shops and an active synagogue. Brooklyn Avenue is now called Cesar Chavez Avenue and the *lingua franca* is Spanish. Street signs are now in Spanish and everyone shops at *el mercado*. The atmosphere seems more Mexican than much of Mexico. A series of circumstances led me to make my home on New Jersey Street, an island of land in the middle of a confluence of LA freeways. When friends asked how I could stand the noise living so near the Hollywood Freeway, I assured them that it wasn't really a problem because the roar of Interstate 10 drowned it out.

Questions of who was legal and who wasn't were not talked about. It was clear that, within families, some had papers and others didn't. A husband might be documented, while his wife was not. Children born in the U.S. might be citizens, but their parents might only have a green card. However, one thing was clear: I was the real immigrant. East LA was their country, papers or no papers. Despite that reality, I was not simply tolerated, but welcomed. The welcome I received often took the form of gifts of food. In fact, I noticed that a competition had developed between the neighbors on either side of me to serve me the most delicious dinner. Tacos, arroz con pollo, carne guisada, savory and sweet tamales, menudo—the tripe soup that I never developed a taste for—and fruit from their gardens all made their way to my doorstep. Never had I felt so welcomed in my entire life.

Shortly after arriving in Arkansas, a study was released that showed that Arkansas had the fastest growing Latino population in the country and that Benton County had the fastest growing Latino population in the state. I was embarrassed that the Christian community had done so little to welcome our new neighbors. I was especially embarrassed that there was not a single worship service in Spanish in the entire Episcopal Diocese of Arkansas and I wanted us to do something about that. I envisioned a day when our coffee-hour tables were not just filled with the beautiful fruits, cheeses, and pastries we typically have, but also with tacos, frijoles, y pan dulce. I imagined us sharing the abundance that we enjoy with our Latino neighbors and I see them enriching our lives by sharing their gifts of the Spirit with us as well.

Focus on Outward Social Transformation

After attending a luncheon at the Boys and Girls Club of Bentonville, a leader in the Hispanic community brought me troubling news. She told me of the growing numbers of children who were being abandoned when their parents, discovered by police or immigration authorities to be without proper documentation, were immediately incarcerated. The situation is very dire. For example, a child can come home from school and find that the parents they love and depend on have simply disappeared. She asked whether we, the community of All Saints' *Todos los Santos,* could be of help to these children. Responding to such a need is one of those chances for rebirth, a movement from darkness to light.

We often come to church seeking renewal. We are uplifted by the music, the oft-repeated prayers touch us in a life-giving way, and you might hear something in a homily worth talking about over lunch. But the movement of the Spirit can flow in the opposite direction as well. When we consciously move through the world, when we go about our daily lives with an awareness of the example of Jesus, who healed the sick, cared for the poor, and reached out to those at the margins of society, we are just as likely to encounter the movement of Spirit there as we are inside these hallowed walls. We are born again when we are in the midst of God's work in the world. Our worship here always runs the risk of becoming rarefied and sterile when it is focused inward. But if our worship is focused on an outward social transformation, we will be fed, nurtured, and constantly renewed.

John tells us of Nicodemus, who asked Jesus, "How can anyone be born after having grown old?" (John 3:4). The opportunity to be born again and to find renewal in the spirit abounds. We only need to emerge from the darkness. Nicodemus' conception of rebirth was narrow. "How can I enter into my mother's womb again?" he asked. Jesus tells him that rebirth takes many forms and can come from any direction. The Spirit moves like the wind and the wind blows where it chooses. If we as a people are to be continually renewed, we must allow the breeze to move us like a sailboat on a silent sea.

Nicodemus, who was a Pharisee, came to Jesus with a particular understanding of what it meant to uphold God's law. It is easy for a church to put together a rigid framework of ideas about what it means to be a follower of Jesus and what it means to worship God. It is easy to get caught up in what constitutes proper worship, whether music should be traditional or contemporary, whether our style is high church or low church, or if we are formal or informal. My prayer is that churches are always alert to the movement of Spirit and that they can be known in a hundred years as places where anyone can be born again, and again, and again.

Certified by Baptism

One afternoon, I received a call from Margarita, a leader in the Hispanic community in Northwest Arkansas. The purpose of her call was to talk with me about the need for children of undocumented immigrants to receive physical examinations at the community clinic. Physicals are a requirement that the school system has for children to enter school. As we talked, she spoke of another concern: Children entering the school system are required to present birth certificates. This sometimes presents a problem for the children of parents without documents. Margarita then mentioned that in lieu of a birth certificate, baptismal certificates are sometimes accepted.

At that moment, I had a vision. I imagined our church's baptismal font positioned on the sidewalk in front of an elementary school on the first day of class. I imagined an alb-clad acolyte holding the cross beside the font as another poured water into the basin while a third held a sign that read: "El Santo Bautismo— Gratis" or "Holy Baptism—Free." Then a line of beautiful five-and-six-year-old children, their dark eyes filled with anticipation and hope, ready to receive the waters of baptism and poised for the chrism that marks them as Christ's own forever. Each of those children would then be presented with a baptismal certificate certifying that the child received the sacrament of Holy Baptism with water, a certificate that also records their date of birth and their parentage, thus granting them entry into an educational system. This sacramental act would thereby proclaim by word and example the Good News of God in Christ that in this world there will be respect for the dignity of every human being. It's a baptismal certificate that acknowledges in Christ there is no outsider, no other, and no need for scapegoats. What is radically different about the formation of a Christian community is that solidarity isn't dependent on the creation of a people that are outside of the love of God. The good news in Christ is that we are all part of the kingdom.

Chosen

One morning, I sat with a young Hispanic woman in the waiting area outside of a courtroom where dozens of defendants awaited their arraignment hearings. As the wheels of justice slowly turned, this was her moment to plead guilty or innocent to the crime of claiming to have a legitimate right to be in this country. The finer points of immigration laws are obscure to her, but she is aware that as one of the undocumented immigrants picked up in the raids on a local restaurant, she will face jail time, deportation, or both.

It is easy for our politicians to call for strict enforcement of immigration laws, claiming that, as they say, "a law is a law." Where is room in that statement for compassion? This young woman has lived in the United States for twelve years; Northwest Arkansas is her home. Her sister, mother, and children live here. Back in Mexico City, only an elderly grandmother remains. She has no friends there, no prospect of a job, and no support network. A life on the streets awaits her. Even worse, she is faced with the awful choice between leaving her children behind, where they stand at least a small chance of living a fruitful life, or taking them with her to share in the utter poverty she faces in a country that is no longer her own. As she talked, I knew that her story is only one single account in a crowd of millions who will suffer from our lack of compassion.

By virtue of being part of this emerging Christian community of All Saints', the entire congregation is part of this evangelical movement as laborers in the harvest with good news to share. Hardly a week passes when I don't receive a phone call from a lost sheep. I can hear the desperation in each voice. People are looking for a place where they can be accepted. These are people who for a whole gamut of reasons have found churches to be inhospitable. And so, we are sent out to the lost sheep. Nothing particularly qualifies us for this work. Peter, Andrew, James, and John weren't qualified either. We simply have good news to share. Progressive church plants like All Saints' are places where everyone is accepted as they are. The fact that there is a place where the harassed and helpless are welcomed is very good news. All of us are called, by word and example, to spread that good news to everyone we encounter. It's not that we are particularly well qualified to do this work. It's just that we, like the twelve, have been chosen for something that is far greater than ourselves.

Workers

For a few years I was a member of the board of directors of a small non-profit organization called the Northwest Arkansas Workers' Justice Center. The center is an advocacy group that works on behalf of a population for whom there are few advocates. The clients are primarily Latino, poor, often undocumented, hardworking, and victims of work injustice. The story of Ignacio Hernandez is typical. Nacho, as he is known, is the principle breadwinner for his family, which includes a young wife and three little girls. Nacho typically works at a variety of construction jobs where he and thousands of other undocumented workers are often cheated by their employers. He came to the Workers' Center when, after spending three days cleaning up a construction site, his employer disappeared without a trace and no one accepted the responsibility of paying Ignacio his wages. Another worker lost his eyesight after being splashed in the face with dangerous chemicals. He had not been provided with safety goggles, nor informed of the hazards of working with the chemicals.

These people, who because of their undocumented status have few of the basic human rights that most Americans take for granted, came to the Workers' Center seeking help. These are the same people of whom Jesus spoke. Those were the very people for whom the prophets Elijah and Elisha were advocates. And it was this very recollection that got Jesus chased out of town. As the Swiss sociologist Max Frisch famously said about his country's immigrants: "We called for workers, and there came human beings."

La Opportunidad

I met Cecilia because she was one of the students in the ESL classes that gather at All Saints' on Tuesday and Thursday evenings. She asked if the two of us could meet together. The next afternoon, Cecilia and I sat down and talked. Through her tears she told me a story of family strife and financial challenges and of a variety of other burdens. Life was difficult for her, but her story was not so very different from the stories it is my privilege to hear from many of the parishioners that attend church on a weekly basis.

As she proceeded to tell me about her children, her tears evaporated and her beautiful smile returned to her face. One of her children is a student at the University of Arkansas. Two others have already graduated and are successfully working in other parts of the country. A single mom for most of their childhood, Cecilia was able to support her children by cleaning houses. Like single mothers all across the country, she came home tired every evening, fed her kids, and made sure they finished all their homework.

Despite having lived in the United States for a total of twenty years, the opportunity to learn English never presented itself. Between the work and the kids, there just simply wasn't any time.

Cecilia didn't come to see me because she was looking for help. On the contrary, Cecilia came to me looking for a way to give. She asked, "¿Hay algo puedo hacer?" or "Is there something I can do?" She was inquiring to know if there was some work she could do at the church on her afternoon off so that she could have "la opportunidad," the opportunity, to practice her English.

Between the Lutherans, the Episcopalians, those who work in the food pantry, and those who prepare the food for our community meal, there is a lot of conversation going on. Now, on most Wednesday afternoons, Cecilia can be found in the kitchen with our cook, Nancy, stirring pots, slicing vegetables, and chatting away in her beautiful, broken English. Cecilia is practicing not just her language skills, but the very essence of what Jesus taught in Matthew 25:40: "Truly I tell you, just as you did it to one of the least of these who are members of my family, you did it to me."

When I look out over the gathered congregation on Sunday, I have to say that it looks a lot like the kingdom of God. But I must ask this question: Are we content to look like God's kingdom? We do present a rather colorful image of what the kingdom is about, but is this just about appearances? I'll be the first to admit that it feels awfully good to be here and soak up the spirit of brotherly and sisterly love that permeates this holy space. Yet, if we are truly to inherit the kingdom of God and not merely look good, we must be about the business of cooking, serving beverages, sewing clothes, nursing, and visiting whomever the least of our extended family may be. We are a people to whom much has been given and from whom much has been required. It is fitting for a community that looks a lot like God's kingdom, to accept the inheritance that we have been offered.

I Am Priest

"Hello, my name is Guillermo Castillo. I am priest." I didn't receive many phone calls from Spanish speakers. When I did, they were usually female and asking about the times for the food bank or looking for the free diapers we handed out for a few Sundays. "I am priest, I was priest at St. Vincent de Paul. You know it, St. Vincent de Paul in Rogers?"

In English, when a priest identifies himself as such he or she will say, "I am a priest." In Spanish, the identifying phrase *Soy sacerdote* literally means "I am priest." Guillermo's statement is more an affirmation of his identity than a mere description of his occupation. It is a statement of his vocation, his calling, and who he is. Guillermo is priest in the same way that someone might say, "I am Italian," rather than the less absolute, "I am an Italian." Or as someone else might say, "I am Christian," rather than "I am a Christian." The latter indicating that one is a member of a group, but the former saying something about how one's identity is wholly linked with Christianity. My first visit with Guillermo convinced me that he was and is priest.

"Yes, of course," I answered. St. Vincent de Paul is a very large Roman Catholic Church in the neighboring town of Rogers, a town with a number of chicken processing plants where many Latinos in the area work.

"You are priest?" he asked.

"That's right," and I identified myself.

"That is good," he said to me as if he needed to tell himself that all was well with this conversation. "You know Anthony Guillén? He said I call you. I want talk with you about church Episcopalian." Anthony Guillén is the director of Latino/Hispanic Ministries in the Episcopal Church. Cindee and I had spent an evening with Anthony giggling over Sara Palin's speech at the Republican National Convention in 2008.

"Sure, I know Anthony, *es un amigo*." At that point I began to speak Spanish. My Spanish isn't very good, but Guillermo and I easily moved, for the first time, into a mode of communication that combined my Spanish and his English. This style eventually became the norm for us. "Good. That is good," replied Guillermo. And much good has resulted from our collaboration since our first encounter.

La Virgen

The Virgin of Guadalupe is given credit, as one Latin American scholar has written, "for bringing together people of distinct cultural heritages, while at the same time affirming their distinctness." On an average Sunday, the pews at All Saints' are occupied by people who have come to Benton County from at least a dozen different countries. And people have come to All Saints' from a myriad different religious traditions as well: Baptists, Methodists, Lutherans, Pentecostals, Mormons, Roman Catholics, Jews, and Muslims. People have come from traditions that were high church and low church and even traditions of no church. Since all have found a home in our midst, it is very fitting that the Virgin of Guadalupe has found a home at All Saints' as well.

At the inaugural Festival of the Virgin of Guadalupe held at All Saints', an expectant crowd totaling about sixty in number gathered in the nave to sing songs of tribute to the Virgin. Our framed portrait of the Virgin of Guadalupe was covered in roses and was mounted on a shiny wooden platform that had earlier seen life as a coffee table. A craftsman had mounted two handles at each end of the platform so that parishioners could carry the Virgin's portrait as if she were the Queen of the Nile rather than the Queen of Heaven. It was a rainy evening, but we marched around the block in a candlelit procession and followed the image of the Virgin while singing songs of joyful adoration, leaving a trail of rose petals on the sidewalks of Central Avenue.

After the Eucharist, Guillermo Castillo, by then our associate vicar, asked two families to come forward. The mothers and their daughters were proudly dressed in the colorful feast day costumes that are characteristic of the indigenous people of Central America. Guillermo's young son, Anthony, or "Mito" as he is usually called, was dressed in a baggy, pajama-like, Mexican peasant costume. Guillermo's wife, Araceli, had penciled in a thin, swooping mustache above Mito's little red lips, so that he resembled a miniature Juan Diego.

As the costumed congregants gathered around the image of Mary, Guillermo took holy water, sprinkled it over them, blessed them, blessed everyone who had gathered, and then called out: "¡*Viva la Virgen de Guadalupe!*" And the people responded, "¡*Viva la Virgen de Guadalupe!*" Then Guillermo exclaimed: "¡*Viva Todos los Santos!*" And the people replied, "¡*Viva Todos los Santos!*" Who could have imagined such an evening in a little Episcopal church in the northwest corner of Arkansas? I'm a strong believer in calling and I think that each of us has been called to something important. All of us are called to give birth to that which is holy and good. The question is: How do we respond to that calling? It may be that God has called you, individually, to a particular task. But God has a habit of calling a people, together, to be an instrument of God's mission on earth.

Progressive church plants carry within their womb the seed of new life. We have each been visited by the angel Gabriel who says, "Greetings, favored ones, The Lord is with you!" It is possible that the planting of a church may be the great summons of our each of our lives. It may be that on the day in which we are called to be with the angels and reflect on what we have accomplished, that this work, in which we are engaged, may be the work of which we are most proud. We are a people pregnant with promise. We hold within us the potential to give birth to all manner of miraculous things. May we have the obedience and the courage to echo Mary's reply by saying, "Here we are, the servants of the Lord; let it be with us according to your word."

Bearing Fruit

The gardener in the parable of the fig tree convinces the land-owner to allow him to dig around the fig tree, put manure on it, and give it another year to bear fruit. How do we know whether the path we have chosen is worth another year's labor in the hope that it will finally bear fruit? All Saints' now has a vibrant and spirit-filled Spanish-speaking portion of our congregation. These folks are a vital and integral part of All Saints'. As I explained to delegates on the floor at a Diocesan Convention, "We don't really do Hispanic ministry any more than we do Anglo ministry; it is just part of who we are." However, it has not always been this way.

Soon after my arrival in Benton County, it was easy for me to see that there was an opportunity for the Episcopal Church to address the needs of a growing Latino community in Northwest Arkansas. I've always had a heart for Latinos, I speak a little Spanish, and the Delacruz family was interested in being involved, so we started celebrating the Holy Eucharist in Spanish. I spent time in *tortillerias* and at the Hispanic Chamber of Commerce, attended soccer games, and went to festivals. I labored for long hours writing sermons that were delivered in pretty awful Spanish. We decided to adjust the service times, invite guest preachers, change the music, advertise to the local Latino community, and showered attention on visitors. We even temporarily changed our location. Throughout it all, the Delacruz family remained faithful, but on a really good day a dozen people would show up at church. After almost two years of holding Spanish services every Sunday, I was ready to give up and cut down the fig tree.

It was about that time that I got the phone call from Guillermo Castillo. He told me the story of how he had been a Roman Catholic priest since he was very young, but as he matured he had decided that he wished to have a wife and raise a family, so he had left the priesthood and sometime later married his wife, Araceli. He wanted to know more about the Episcopal Church. Our conversation that day eventually led down a new path, which returned him to the priesthood and resulted in the flourishing community that *Todos los Santos* is today. I like to say that Guillermo fell in love, so he became an Episcopalian. I actually like to say that about everyone's journey to All Saints'. We didn't cut down the fig tree and now we have an orchard, bearing sweet ripe figs for everyone to enjoy.

Bearing Witness to Miracles

The need for Hispanic ministry was apparent to me when I first arrived in Arkansas. Those we minister to are immigrants who live in an oftentimes hostile environment. Their spiritual, emotional, and cultural needs are not being fully addressed by existing churches. So, with more faith than wisdom, we began to hold worship services in Spanish. The music was uncertain, the preaching faltered, and attendance started low and stayed that way. We changed locations, adjusted the time, and tried one idea after another. We were plagued with deportation, disappearance, and indifference. We eventually decided to suspend holding the services in order to regroup. With few results from over an entire year's worth of labor, we could have easily echoed Simon's words: "Master, we have worked all night long but have caught nothing."

And then, after a year of inquiries and conversations and with the blessing of the bishop, our friend Guillermo Castillo joined our communion. Under Guillermo's leadership, we have put out into the deep water and let down our nets yet again. Despite the ice and snow, thirty-eight people showed up for the Spanish service, which was more than twice as many as any previous service. I was tempted, like Simon Peter, to fall down on my knees. It was enough to make a preacher schooled in the historical Jesus of Marcus Borg, the contextual world of John Dominic Crossan, and the cynicism of John Shelby Spong to believe in miracles. I don't know how this endeavor will turn out. I'm realistic enough to know that catching one fine mess of fish does not establish our career as fishermen. And I know that the people who attended Guillermo's first service at Todos Los Santos weren't simply a homogeneous school of fish; they are individuals from Honduras, El Salvador, Mexico, and the Dominican Republic, to name but a few of the represented countries.

When we first started meeting at Washington Junior High School, we were a loosely organized church. I was always hopeful that the backdrops and props that remained on the stage from the previous night's theatre performance would enhance and not distract from the service. We never knew if the bell that signaled students to change classes would go off during our prayers or at communion. I was often uncertain whether anyone would read the lessons until they were actually read.

The rebirthing of our Spanish service reminded me of the early days of All Saints'. First-time visitors enthusiastically became readers and prayers. Our two acolytes, Audrey and Kimberly, had received acolyte training earlier in the week and were ready to serve, but we needed a third. Then I noticed Victor, his slender body almost hidden by the crush of family surrounding him on the pew outside the door. "Would you like to carry the cross?" I asked. He hesitated only a moment before nodding his assent.

Before he could change his mind, I gave him three minutes of acolyte training and whisked him upstairs, torchbearers in tow. We found an alb to fit his slight frame, showed him how to fasten the snaps and knot the cincture. His cousin then lowered a green ribboned cross over his head and carefully centered it on his chest. Instinctively, he stopped at the mirror to inspect the transformation. We left the sacristy and walked toward the stairwell. Just as he took the first step in descent toward the nave, Victor looked up at me and said, "I feel special."

Now, I'm not really sure how to define a miracle, but sometimes I know one when I see one. When this ten-year-old boy, a motherless child raised by his older sister, was made to feel special, it was nothing short of miraculous. If we had done nothing else that wintry day but allow Victor to don the alb of an acolyte and lift high the cross of Jesus, it was surely a day well spent.

Everyone comes to church for all kinds of reasons. I don't really know if one reason is better than another, but I do know that one really good reason for us to gather together is so that we can learn to recognize miracles, to be ready to see them and call them out to one another so that they don't slip past us. For what is a miracle but an encounter with the holy? If we can learn what it feels like to be in the presence of God, it becomes more likely that when we are outside the hallowed walls of a church, we will see what is holy in the world as well. "When they had brought their boats to shore, they left everything and followed him." The bearing of witness to miracles is a call to discipleship.

None of us have been called to the mission of All Saints' or any other progressive church plant because the liturgy is flawless, the music always harmonious, the preaching poetic, or the building an architectural masterpiece. Each of us has been called to climb into this leaky boat together because we, like Simon and the sons of Zebedee, have been chosen to be disciples of Christ. Inside this boat, we are granted the opportunity to witness miracles and then we are asked to leave everything and follow him. Do not be afraid for, from now on, we will be catchers of people.

Who Is My Neighbor?

The parable of the Good Samaritan is understood in popular culture to be a lesson in providing aid to the unfortunate stranger. In Luke's Gospel, the story illustrates Jesus's reply to the lawyer's question "Who is my neighbor?" The answer to this question offers us a profound statement about the nature of love and neighborliness. It was certainly a powerful story for Jesus's listeners. The Samaritans were a despised people. Neither completely Jew nor Gentile, the Samaritans were undesired immigrants in the land of Israel. The entire parable, especially if it includes the conversation between Jesus and the lawyer about neighbors and love, demonstrates how love arises in unanticipated places and how we can learn about life and love from sources that might surprise us.

Some might think that love and law don't mix. But this lawyer, trained in the art of making fine legal distinctions, was attempting to determine legally who the outspoken prophet Jesus thought should be considered a neighbor and thus worthy of love. Jesus's reply to the man who asked, "Who is my neighbor?" contains within it the parable of the Good Samaritan. As the story unfolds, Jesus turns the question of who deserves our love completely upside down. Instead of passing judgment on the legal boundaries of compassion, the actions of the Samaritan tell us that we are to seek out neighbors to receive our love, even when barriers of prejudice or legal distinctions might tell us otherwise. The Samaritan in this parable is the one who sets the example. The Samaritan, the alien, the undesirable, is the one from whom the upstanding citizen, the man most concerned with the law, has the most to learn. The outsiders are the one from whom we learn; they are our teachers.

In the summer of 2010, an historical event unfolded in the life of All Saints'. For the first time ever, the English and Spanish speaking communities of All Saints'/Todos los Santos came together to celebrate the Eucharist as one community. In fact, it was an even more historic occasion for the larger Episcopal Church, as All Saints' is home to the largest bilingual gathering of Episcopalians in the history of the Diocese of Arkansas. After having read the parable of the Good Samaritan, it would be tempting for the congregation of All Saints' to pat themselves on their collective back. They have opened their doors to the Latino community in ways that few other congregations in the area have. Moreover, they have expanded the boundaries of who the average Benton County resident might consider to be their neighbor. The Good Samaritan in this story isn't just the exemplar of one who shows kindness and compassion toward the stranger. The Samaritan is the one who offers the lesson about the true nature of love.

Our 1:00 p.m. Spanish service each Sunday is unlike most every other Anglo church I've attended, where most of the congregation sits at the middle or toward the back. At this service, the Spanish-speaking members gather together at the front. It is indicative of an eagerness to hear the gospel and to share in the good news of the love of Christ. It's always crowded at the front, where people seek the closeness of family and community. Furthermore, it seems that there is a gathering after church almost every week at the home of a parishioner, demonstrating an eagerness to form community and to share in one another's lives. The Spanish service is growing rapidly, simply because the people invite their friends, their neighbors, their family, and their coworkers to join them for worship. And most don't miss a Sunday, unless, of course, a Latin American country or Spain is playing in the World Cup. The closeness of Latino families is well known, often the envy of Anglo parents whose children are geographically and emotionally distant.

It takes an immense amount of courage for these people to leave behind a country they once knew to come settle in this foreign and often hostile land. It was the same kind of admirable courage that many of our forefathers and mothers also exhibited only a few generations back. The industriousness and willingness to work hard is easily recognized in the Hispanic community. One of our parishioners who started doing clothing repairs in her home now employs ten people who do alterations for department stores and dress shops. Another member bought a used tortilla machine and now manufactures tortillas and corn chips and distributes them to four states, meeting a demand for fresher goods with fewer preservatives. These are people who have the courage to start a business when an employer won't hire them.

Contained within the story of the Good Samaritan is a call to show compassion toward those who need it the most. But the larger message for us is to open our eyes to the teacher that has appeared in an unexpected place. Our vision of what it means to be Christian is expanded by our encounter with the immigrant. We can learn from the immigrant who we are as God's people and we can discover new ways to share the love of Christ with others.

On his first visit to All Saints', Bishop Benfield had a conversation before the service with the members that were to be either confirmed or received that day. He asked what had drawn them to All Saints'. The reply of one of the confirmands was, "So that I could be among like-minded people." He meant that he enjoyed being around those who were open-minded, accepting, and inclusive. However, in his wisdom, the bishop replied, "You know, we aren't all necessarily like-minded in the Episcopal Church. We often don't think alike, act alike, or look alike. When we are at our best, we celebrate our differences and find common ground in worshiping together." We gather to lift up one another in love, to celebrate our diversity, and to learn how to love from each other. We learn to love in new ways, not just in spite of our differences, but also because of our differences.

The lawyer who confronted Jesus asked who his neighbor was so that he might know what the law required of him. Instead of learning that the limits of charity are reserved for family, tribe, or those in close proximity, the lawyer learned that the love of neighbors knows no boundaries; the love of God is limitless. Jesus affirmed what the lawyer already knew. If you want to truly live, then love God, love yourself, and love your neighbor.

CHAPTER 11

Who Do You Love?

Set me as a seal upon your heart, as a
seal upon your arm; for love is strong
as death, passion fierce as the grave. Its
flashes are flashes of fire, a raging flame.
Many waters cannot quench love, neither
can floods drown it.

—Song of Solomon 8:6–7

After viewing the website for the local organization called the
Gay, Lesbian, Bisexual, Transgender Community, I called
one of the directors. "Hello," a voice hesitatingly answered.
"Hi. My name is Roger Joslin, I am an Episcopal priest." I some-
times claimed to be a priest among non-Episcopalians, when, in fact,
I was a deacon awaiting ordination to the priesthood. Explaining the

intricacies of the transitional diaconate, versus the permanent diaconate, seems to confuse more than clarify. In this world of Baptists,
the deacon is the old guy who makes the business decisions in a church
so that the well-meaning but inept young pastor doesn't get the church
in financial hot water. Since the small town folks have a vague idea
of what a priest does, I settled on introducing myself as a priest to
avoid any unnecessary confusion. Though there is an ingrained suspicion of the office, the role is mysterious enough to command some
measure of interest, if not respect. "I am new in Bentonville and I
am starting an Episcopal church," I continued. "The church will be
inclusive, the kind of place where you will be welcomed whether you
are black or brown, rich or poor, gay or straight. It is important that
all kinds of people be involved in the formation of the church from
the very beginning. I would like to talk with you about the gay and
lesbian community being part of what we are planning."

"That sounds interesting," the voice offered.

"Would you like to get together for lunch or coffee or something
and talk about it?"

"Yeah, I think so, but I would like for other members of the
board to be there."

"That sounds good to me. When would you like to get together?"
I asked, hoping we could get started soon.

"I don't know, maybe Monday. Can I call you back?"

"Sure, give me a call."

In my persistent way, I didn't wait for her call back. Instead, I
e-mailed her and told her how much I had enjoyed the conversation
and that I was looking forward to hearing from her. She e-mailed me
back suggesting a time and place. The following Monday, I met with
Carol, Kay, and John. The three of them sat at a small table together,
an assortment of papers and pamphlets scattered across the surface.
They had spotted me through the glass exterior walls as I walked
across the plaza leading to the coffee shop and they used the time it
took for me to find them to look me over. By the time my eyes rested
on the three of them, they were smiling at me. With very kind eyes,
Carol looked at me and spoke up, "You must be Roger."

"I wasn't sure that I would recognize you, but I was reasonably certain you would recognize me," I said. I was dressed in black from head to toe, except for the single strip of white wrapped around my neck that formed my clerical collar.

Conversation with them was easy. They told me how difficult it is to connect with people in the gay community in Bentonville. There are no gay bars in the area, except for a few in Fayetteville. Thus, they were inspired to establish a center where the LGBT community could gather safely and securely and they wanted their own building because they did not want to place others in a position where they might be in danger.

The three of them were raised in the church, coming from the Baptist and Church of Christ traditions. When Kay came out to her family, they had threatened to have her kidnapped and sent to a place in Oklahoma where she would be brainwashed into believing that being gay is a sinful disorder. Kay informed her mother that if she followed through with those plans, she would have her arrested.

Her mother responded, "Kay, you wouldn't have your own mother arrested!"

"Mom, you wouldn't have your own daughter kidnapped, would you?" As it turned out, no one was arrested or kidnapped and now they simply don't speak of it anymore.

Kay told me that she wanted to be a foster parent, but on the application form there is a line that asked whether the applicant is gay or lesbian. She indicated on the form that she was. The interviewer asked her if she was a "practicing homosexual."

Kay responded, "Not right now, but if I meet someone, I might be."

Learning this, the interviewer replied, "Then you are disqualified from participating in the program, by state law." Kay left the meeting heartbroken.

Carol then recounted to me a case in Bentonville in which a mother was having her children taken from her because she was in a same-sex relationship. I thought to myself: "Can this really be true?"

As they began to trust me, the conversation flowed more easily. I told them of our plans for an inclusive church: "I envision this as the kind of place where you can feel comfortable sitting in the pews holding hands with your partner; where you can adopt a child and find a community that will embrace you and your child. In order to ensure that the church develops along those lines, I want to include members of the LGBT community in its early formation. We don't have to change to accept you. We will be an inclusive community from the beginning, if you are a part of it."

I asked if they thought the LGBT community would be interested in being a part of an Episcopal church in Bentonville. The three of them felt very confident that the LGBT community would be receptive since they were even excited about it themselves. I expressed my desire to form a group that could explore what it means to be gay and a Christian. In return, they invited me to attend the next meeting at the center and make a pitch to the guests.

An Expanding Circle of Compassion

One of my parishioners was walking with a colleague down the halls of their workplace when they encountered Jim, another member of All Saints'. Introductions were made and they all chatted amicably. With the recent Supreme Court rulings on same-sex marriage in the news that day, the colleague asked how our church could justify gay marriage. The parishioner promptly responded, "Well, Jim is gay and married."

I have occasionally been drawn into "proof-texting" conversations where in response to quotes from Leviticus about "abominations" and the sin of "a man lying with a man," I am likely to bring up other biblical prohibitions against eating shellfish, or wearing clothes of mixed fabrics, or borrowing or lending money with interest, all laws that we now disregard with impunity. When my fundamentalist friends quote scripture attributed to the Apostle Paul that seems to regard homosexuality as idolatrous, I've sometimes noted how Paul was a product of his times and, as such, also failed to condemn slavery and frequently regarded women as less than equal. I might also point out that I am a follower of Jesus, who had nothing to say about same-sex relations.

Truthfully, I doubt that I have ever persuaded anyone who wasn't ready to be convinced that, in the eyes of God, one's sexual orientation is of no consequence. Neither have I successfully persuaded a skeptic that God blesses all kinds of loving relationships, both gay and straight. However, what I have observed is that hearts and minds are often changed by personal encounters with people. Relationships can uproot even the most deeply held prejudices. The workplace encounter with Jim, and the discovery that this decent, intelligent, thoroughly likable man was not only gay, but was part of a healthy, enduring, and committed relationship with another man, chipped away at the idea that the bond between two loving human beings can only take a particular form.

At All Saints', we have same-sex couples that have been together for over forty years. We have gay couples that have successfully raised beautiful children to adulthood. I have witnessed the genuine grief of men and women whose same-sex partners have unexpectedly passed away. I've watched same-sex couples care for one another through crisis and grave illness. And I have shared the joy of gay and lesbian people who have found, to both their surprise and delight, that the church can be a place where they will not be judged according to their sexual preference.

I have seen old prejudices fall away as parents observe a lesbian couple bring Bible stories to life for their children in a Sunday school classroom. I have watched a gruff old man, with the prejudices of his generation, be transformed by the simple experience of cooking barbeque, side by side, with a man he learned was gay. Full participation by the gay and lesbian community in church councils, guilds, choirs, and committees all provide opportunities for transformation and for the melting away of past prejudices.

People in heterosexual relationships who attend church regularly may continue to label same-sex relationships as sinful, despite the June 2015 ruling that same-sex marriage has the same legitimacy as opposite-sex marriage. My personal encounter with dozens of gay and lesbian couples has convinced me that these relationships contain within them all the joy and all the challenge that can be found in every relationship. Who are we to stand in the way of God's desire to bless all creation?

I have heard it said that the Emancipation Proclamation granted freedom, not only to the slave, but to the slave owner who was freed from the shackles that bound him as well. The slave owner found liberation from active participation in a system of domination and injustice that prevented him from treating fellow human beings with respect and dignity. I think that a similar kind of liberation will take place now that marriage equality has become the law of the land. We can no longer deny justice and equality for same-sex couples that seek to be married. Nor can we allow our own prejudices to prevent us from fully embracing God's vision of universal love. How can we allow our own prejudices, our own narrow conception of the way that life and love should be ordered, to place limits on the imagination of God?

Over the years, I have heard dozens of stories of gays and lesbians in this community who grew up in the church and their yearning to be a part of a Christian community persists. However, the church rejects them, or at best, allows them into their congregation, but condemns their "sinful lifestyle" and insists that they change.

One day, I was invited to have lunch with the associate pastor of First Presbyterian Church. Since it is the church where Sam and Helen Walton once attended, First Presbyterian is well known in the area. The pastor had seen an article in the paper about the progressive church I was planting in Bentonville and he wanted to extend a heartfelt welcome to me. He had attended Austin Presbyterian Theological Seminary and indicated that he was sympathetic to my efforts to combat racism and homophobia. He told me of First Presbyterian's initiative to allow two gay men to join their church. The senior pastor decided to prepare the congregation by leading a class in which issues of homosexuality were explored. The couple was finally admitted to the church. However, despite the great lengths taken for preparation, ten families left and the couple never felt accepted by the congregation. Tragically, one of the men died from complications from AIDS and the other eventually left the church feeling rejected, misunderstood, and abandoned. The associate pastor asked for my card so that he could point the man in my direction in the hopes that he could find a home at All Saints'.

No One Leaves Hungry

One afternoon, I received a phone call from a lesbian couple who were looking for a church in which to raise their daughter without recrimination. They spoke about joining the church with the pastor of a downtown church affiliated with the denomination of their youth. The pastor told them that they could visit, but they needed to keep a low profile and not reveal the nature of their relationship. He suggested a six-month probationary period to see if "they would be accepted by the congregation." They were sent away hungry. Their story of conditional acceptance made me want to weep.

I later spoke with the pastor who had sent them away. He explained that he was sympathetic to the needs of the couple, but in his previous posting, the "gay issue" had nearly torn his church apart and he wasn't going to let that happen again. May we never become a church that parcels out its love, offering it to some while withholding it from others. When Jesus and the disciples fed the five thousand, he didn't instruct the disciples to give bread to those who seemed to deserve it or to those that met particular cultural, theological, or sociological conditions. Instead, he simply broke the bread, blessed it, and fed everyone. In fact, this large scale feeding was part of the miracle. All these different people sat down together and shared the loaves and fishes. It is a miracle that progressive church plants like All Saints' can gather a collection of strangers and form them into a community that is committed to learning how to love.

Jesus could have told his disciples: "Let's garner our resources. We don't really have enough to feed our own. Send the crowd away and let them fend for themselves." However, this was not the case. Jesus said, "They need not go away; you give them something to eat." May no one ever leave church hungry.

The identity of a progressive church plant, its personality, and its sense of self is being formed by its early membership. My prayer is that because of the work being done today, fifty years from now progressive churches like All Saints' will be known as places where no one leaves hungry, where everyone is fed, and where God's love is shared with everyone who walk through its doors.

Courage to Love

A few years into my tenure in Bentonville, it was, with great sorrow, my privilege to preside at the burial service of a much-loved gay parishioner. The following is an excerpt from the homily:

> As most every one of you gathered here today knows, it takes courage to love. To love another person is to place yourself in a uniquely vulnerable position. The love you offer to someone else may not be reciprocated. The person you love may choose to love another. Or it may be that the expectation that you will cherish another, "till death do us part," will be cut short by the vagaries of accident or ill health. This is the ordinary kind of courage it takes to love another. It takes courage of an altogether different order of magnitude to love as Joe loved. Let's be honest, we live in a beautiful part of the country, filled with people that are beautiful and good-hearted as well. But it is also a land of bigotry, racism, homophobia, and hate. This is a very difficult place to establish and maintain a same-sex

relationship. But for Joe, this was home. And this is where, in his own quiet way, he took a stand against hate on behalf of love.

Since coming to Northwest Arkansas, I've learned something about changing hearts and minds. Eloquent sermons, fiery newspaper columns, and noisy demonstrations do little to turn around narrow-mindedness. Narrow-mindedness, by definition, isn't touched by persuasive argument. What changes hearts and minds is personal interaction with someone whose way of living and being in the world flies in the face of previously held conceptions of what is possible and good. Because Joe had the courage to follow love, his family, friends, and everyone he encountered had their old prejudices challenged and nudged in the direction of tolerance, acceptance, and understanding.

How is prejudice overcome? Not usually by legislation, lobbying, or debate. Not by demonstration of sound theological understanding or by Bible thumping, proof texting, or sociological studies. Joe offered evidence that God can bless all sorts of relationships. It's not that his relationships were perfect. They were often tumultuous just like mine and yours. Going about the simple business of loving others, Joe showed the world that the love of God knows no bounds. Our highest and best tribute to Joe, our recognition that his life was not lived in vain, is for us to love deeply as well, and to bless love wherever it appears.

CHAPTER 12

A Captive Congregation

From heaven the LORD looked at the earth, to hear the groans of the prisoners.

—Psalm 102:19–20

I'm convinced that Jesus wept when he read the paper in 2008 and learned that, for the first time in U.S. history, we incarcerate one in a hundred Americans. And when I drove up to the Benton County jail a few days later, I passed the sign that proclaims (proudly or with shame, I'm not sure) that the inmate population that day was 512. There is just enough room at the bottom of the sign for the words "Jesus wept." Numbers like that don't mean so much to us, until they represent someone we love, until someone we know and care about personally passes endless days behind steel bars. And then we, along with Jesus, shed our tears.

My first encounter with the Benton County Sheriff's Department was a telephone call I made to inquire about the purpose of a sign in front of the jail proclaiming the number of inmates housed inside. The sheriff's deputy, with whom I spoke, voiced surprise at my inquiry. He indignantly claimed that the new electronic sign out front had been his idea adding, "No one has ever complained about it before." In response to our conversation, I decided to use my newspaper column that week as a platform to bring the sign to the public's attention. The column, published on February 13, 2010, reads as follows:

> If you are driving west on Highway 102, a few blocks past Walton Boulevard, you are greeted with a friendly electronic billboard informing you of the time and temperature and, as it announced last Tuesday afternoon, a Benton County Inmate Population of 482. I've been bewildered by this sign for some time. When I first noticed the sign in its earlier wooden form, before it was replaced by the new digitized version, I wasn't certain about the sheriff department's motive in displaying the number of prisoners housed within the jail's walls. My first thought was that there must be a county regulation requiring that the number of people we keep in the county jail be displayed for all the public to see. It seems, after all, a matter of great shame, and we probably should be constantly reminded of how many young men and women we have given up on and decided to lock away.
>
> But, sadly, I fear that the number of people kept in the Benton County jail is a point of pride for our jailers. The county grimly proclaims the growing number of human beings held captive within the jail's cold grey walls with the same satisfaction that the Walmart Home Office boasts of saving families $33 billion or the way McDonald's used to brag about how many million hamburgers they've sold.

I wonder at what point we, like McDonald's, will consider the number of people locked behind bars to be too many to count. Or will we eventually realize that imprisoning ever-larger numbers of human beings is no solution to crime?

One of the earliest and most enduring impressions I formed of Benton County was the sight of young men and women, wearing striped uniforms and stooping over to pick up our trash in the grassy median along Interstate 540. Striped prison uniforms, commonly used in the nineteenth century, were largely abolished in the United States early in the twentieth century because their continued use as a badge of shame was considered undesirable. Apparently, shame has made a comeback in Benton County.

And perhaps even more appalling than the shameful public display of Benton County's numerical contribution to the indecent act of warehousing human beings is our county's light-hearted attitude toward incarceration. On the electronic billboard outside the jailhouse is the graphic depiction of a cartoonish figure dressed in the same humiliating, horizontally-striped prison garb our county prisoners are forced to wear and dragging a ball and chain across the face of the sign. Ask any sorrowful family who has a child or father locked away behind those grim walls if they think that the Chaplainesque figure on the sign is the least bit funny.

We act as if jailing so many of our fellow citizens is an acceptable practice. In the United States, we have an incarceration rate that is many times the rate of most European countries. No country in the world jails as many of its citizens as we do. For the first time in the nation's history, more than one in a hundred American adults are behind bars. Almost one quarter of the people who are imprisoned worldwide are in U.S. jails. We lock up people for crimes that most countries consider minor civil offenses or treatable afflictions. Sentences are long and parole is limited. Our bail bond system is among the most unjust elements of our criminal justice system, keeping thousands of people in jail while they await trial. Nationwide we spend about $24,000 a year to keep a person in prison. That's more than twice as much as the Bentonville School District spends to educate a child.

As long as elected judges and law enforcement officials consider the number of our children they place behind bars to be a point of pride and evidence of a job well done, then we, as a society, have failed. We should elect politicians who promise to keep people out of jails, not put more inside. The entire prison system is a hell on earth that we have unleashed upon ourselves. Lives are ruined. Families are torn apart and destroyed. Freedom is denied and justice is parceled out in a manner that favors the rich and condemns the poor and minorities. Perhaps the next time we drive by the county jail, we should remember that the steadily rising numbers on the sign out front represent, not just prisoners, not merely detainees, but our children—God's children. And by heaping ridicule on those we lock away we bring great shame, not just on the law-breakers we intend to shame, but on ourselves as well.

Inside

I first visited the Benton County Jail to meet with the grandson of a parishioner. Visitors arriving at the jail are faced with the decision to enter one of two formidable entrances. The double door to the right leads to the sheriff's office and the door to the left leads, eventually, to the jail. By taking the left-hand entrance, I passed in front of two rows of metal chairs occupied by jail visitors. Those who had come to the jail were mostly the families of the inmates: talkative young women holding babies and sad-eyed parents. A metal desk sits in the corner where a bondsman explains the need for cash or a money order.

The rules for visitation are posted on the bulletin board:

1. Dress code for women: only conservatively dressed ladies will be allowed to visit inmates.
2. You must leave a state-issued ID in order to visit.
3. Only four people are allowed to visit an inmate at a time.

A soundproof glass wall erected beside an airport-style metal detector reveals an office staff, more spiritless than most, whose main occupation seems to be to ignore those they are charged to oversee. I stood at the counter and waited about a minute for the uniformed clerk to attend to the paperwork task on her desk. "Can I help you?" she asked, without laying down her pencil or looking up at me.

"I have an appointment to see James McAlester," I replied.

She listlessly reviewed the database on her computer, or perhaps just continued her game of solitaire. "Could I see your state-issued ID?"

With a hand lever, the clerk opened the jaws of a plastic cylinder imbedded in the countertop between us and I dropped my Arkansas driver's license inside. The jaws snapped shut, the cylinder rotated, and the mouth opened to reveal its contents to the clerk. She removed the license and kept her eyes trained on it while entering the information it provided into her database. Something of mild interest must have been revealed to her, or so I surmised judging by her quick glance upward at me before lowering her eyes again. After collecting all the information she needed, the clerk said, "The guard will call your name in a few minutes."

As promised, five minutes later the guard called out through an intercom, "Mr. Joslin." I rose from my seat. "Please walk slowly through the metal detector." After I passed through the detector, the guard directed me through another door, behind which was arranged a series of booths with a smudged glass wall positioned to separate visitors from prisoners. Phones were hanging on the partitions that divided each booth. The hum in the room was reminiscent of the background noise one often hears from a Mumbai call center, but this time with an Arkansas accent.

The young man was waiting for me, smiling, more cheerful than I expected or was warranted by his grim circumstances. He was thinner than I remembered. We each picked up our phones. The conversation was light and a little stilted. "They treating you okay?" I asked.

"It's all right. It's hard to sleep. The lights are on all the time," he responded.

"How's the food?"

"Awful. Just sandwiches. Three times a day. You get a little sick of them."

I was floored. "You've been in here three weeks and you've only eaten sandwiches?"

"Guys are in here years and only eat sandwiches," he replied.

That's the part of our conversation that I carried home with me. I did some checking and discovered that other inmates told me the same story. I called the sheriff's office to check and the jail captain politely confirmed that this was the jail policy. He offered to provide me with a copy of the menu if I filled a request under the "Freedom of Information Act." The jail captain told me that he would have a copy of the menu waiting for me if I came by the next day.

As I approached the jail the next morning, I expected to see the electronic sign usually proudly proclaiming the number of prisoners occupying cells in the county jail. Instead, the sheriff, apparently anticipating my arrival, had prepared a digitized greeting for me: "Menu Today: Breakfast: bologna sandwiches; Lunch: bologna sandwiches; Dinner: bologna sandwiches." I had intended to merely pick up a copy of the menu, but I took the jail's signage as an invitation to meet personally with the sheriff. Approaching the glass-encased receptionist's area, I identified myself and said, "I'm here to pick up a copy of the jail menu I requested."

"Just a moment," she replied. Within a few minutes, she returned with a copy of the menu and passed it to me through an opening at the base of the glass wall separating us.

"Thank you," I offered and then asked, "Would it be possible to speak with the sheriff?"

For the first time, the receptionist looked up at me and studied my face. After a long pause, she replied, "I'll check." I sat for about ten minutes in one of the chrome and plastic chairs, suitably chosen to furnish the cinderblock-lined office.

Eventually, I heard the electronic lock on the door switch open and a young man with chiseled features and a healthy complexion that belied the long hours he spent indoors guarding prisoners reached out his hand and politely introduced himself as the jail captain. "I understand that you would like to see the sheriff," he said.

"That's right," I said.

"Then come with me."

We walked briefly down a corridor and through the open door leading to the sheriff's office. Without looking up at me, the sheriff continued to talk with a half-dozen armed deputies, all standing around the sheriff's desk while he leaned back in his chair and issued directives to each of them. When he finished, the silent deputies filed past me and out of the room, not one of them acknowledging my presence.

I can't remember now if the sheriff was wearing the felt Stetson hat that was atop his head in the large framed picture that adorned the jail lobby walls. Surely, he didn't. He wasn't of a generation of men that casually wore hats indoors. But there was something about his deliberate desire to project an image of authority that made me imagine that he always wore his Stetson in much the same way that a John Wayne character might tilt his hat back on his head just to make a point, but would seldom actually take it off.

"Have a seat," he said in the tone of a man more accustomed to giving orders than making requests. "What's on your mind?"

I answered, "The food served to the prisoners. Sandwiches, three times a day? Never a hot meal? That seems wrong to me."

"Look," he said, "I'm not running a country club. The people in here did something wrong, sometimes awful things to kids, and I'm not here to coddle them."

"But many of the people in the jail have not been convicted of anything. You have taken it upon yourself to punish them. A diet of sandwiches is just not healthy."

"They get fruit, and carrot sticks," he reached for the menu, "and celery and a dairy drink." His face was reddening and I could see that the jail captain, who had remained behind and sat at the small conference table with us, was glancing nervously first at my face and then at the sheriff's.

I replied, "And never a hot meal—even if they stay here a year. I treat my dogs better."

The sheriff placed his palms flat on the table and rose slightly from his seat, leaning toward me. Involuntarily, I found myself assuming the same posture, leaning toward him until our faces were only inches apart. "Don't you ever, ever, try to tell me how to run my jail," he spat out his words.

I'm neither particularly brave, nor confrontational, but something in the moment prevented me from succumbing to the sheriff's attempt at intimidation. Perhaps it is because, growing up in Texas, I was accustomed to the demeanor of the small-town sheriff. Or perhaps, speaking on behalf of the marginalized gave me the strength I needed. Or maybe, truth be told, I was just being arrogant myself. Whatever the source, I returned the sheriff's intense gaze and said, "Sheriff, this isn't your jail. You work for the people of Benton County, people like me. This isn't your jail and these are not your prisoners to treat however you wish."

The jail captain had risen in his seat as well, not so much to referee, but in readiness to remove the sheriff's hands from my throat in case he attempted to throttle me. I took a deep breath and then another, loud enough to allow the sheriff to hear the rhythm of my breathing. I settled back into my seat and he did the same. We continued to hold each other's gaze while we breathed in unison.

"Look," he said, "the people that elected me expect me to be tough on prisoners. If they aren't happy with the work I'm doing, they can elect someone else. I've got nothing to hide. If you would like to see the jail, my captain can show you around."

"I'd like that," I said. We didn't part friends, but we did shake hands and I think we understood each other.

Incarcerating the Christ

One icy morning, I stood at the kitchen sink long enough to allow the water from the tap to heat up, so that when it splashed onto my puppies' dry dog food, the combination of warm water and kibbles synthesized into a brownish, if rather thin, chunk-filled gravy. The dogs always show me their appreciation for my slight efforts by quickly gobbling their chow and licking their bowls to a clean shine. Sometimes I imagine that they look up from their dishes long enough to cast a smile in my direction.

Some mornings I'm in a hurry and I fail to take the time to heat the water. The dogs eat their breakfast anyway and the nutrients are the same, warm or cold. But on those days when I know that my wife and I will both be gone and the dogs must spend long hours left alone in their cages away from the people they are close to, I like to know that they at least have the memory of a warm meal.

It's a small thing, really, and hardly worth noting. Yet, it's likely that many people, who also love their pets, engage in similar practices of providing small comforts to their animals. And so it was, watching the steam rise from my dog's bowl, that I recalled the previous day's conversation with yet another former resident of the Benton County jail, one who reminded me that prisoners in the local jail never receive a hot meal.

Whether a person is locked away for a few days, or remains in jail for a few years, he or she will never receive a hot meal. If your neighbor wrote a hot check to buy groceries for her children, if the son of the deacon in your church is arrested for possession of marijuana, and if your nephew is locked up for driving under the influence of alcohol, they will be served cold food for the entire length of their stay. I don't mean that the meatloaf, mashed potatoes, and green beans that you may be planning to feed your family one evening has cooled to room temperature as it is transferred from the jail's kitchen to the prisoners' plates. I mean that, by design, every single day, the young men and women in the local jail are fed cold cereal for breakfast, a cold sandwich for lunch, and another cold sandwich for dinner.

The sheriff informed me that the practice of feeding mostly processed meat and white bread to prisoners was passed down to him by the previous administration and that he simply continued the practice. The sheriff also told me that, other than the prisoners themselves, I am only the second person during his tenure in office to voice opposition to the unusual custom of denying prisoners hot food. I can only imagine that the reason he has not heard loud opposition is that the good people of Benton County are unaware of the practice.

We are all better than this. For the people who reside in the hometown of the largest corporation in the world, the home to some of the richest people on the planet, to allow the least among us to suffer is a matter of shame for all of us. There are many things vying for the attention of compassionate people of faith. Abject poverty, social injustice, joblessness, and issues of war and peace cry out for our attention. And knowing how to tackle those big issues can be so overwhelmingly complex. Instead of grappling with their complexity, we often do nothing. Occasionally, an issue presents itself that is not difficult to understand. Even those in disparate faith communities, who agree on little, can understand and accept that common decency requires that we adequately feed those in desperate circumstances, those who are entrusted to our care.

A few months ago it was proposed that the prisoners in the Benton County jail be permitted to work in vegetable gardens. At first, that seems like a good idea, allowing those normally confined to cages to flex their muscles, dig in the earth, and enjoy a little fresh air. Yet the irony of the practice is inescapable. Can we, in good conscience, permit our imprisoned to grow vegetables that they can never eat, to sow where they will never harvest? In Matthew 25, Jesus speaks of a king who told his subjects that whenever they fed the hungry, welcomed the stranger, clothed the naked, or visited the imprisoned they had done those things to him as well. If this is true, we've incarcerated the Christ. The least we can do is serve him a hot meal.

Three Prayers

I cannot recount the number of times I've attended banquets, public meetings, and assemblies of various kinds that have started out with some preacher's idea of a prayer of thanksgiving. It's typically something like: "I just want to thank you Jesus, or I just want to thank you, Father God, for all the blessings you have bestowed on us in Northwest Arkansas." It is as if the guy praying thinks that out of all the places in the world, God has chosen to grant some special blessing on the land of Walmart, Tyson, and J.B. Hunt. And he is making sure that God knows that we are grateful.

As a member of the Bentonville Ministerial Alliance, I was asked to occasionally pray at the beginning of the monthly Quorum Court meeting. The Quorum Court is composed of a group of justices of the peace, elected by the citizens of Benton County, and is responsible for the upkeep of county roads and various environmental issues, and allocates funding for the county jail operations. In 2012, I prayed on three separate occasions.

In January I prayed for the prisoners: "Gracious One, We are thankful for today's life-giving rain and sunshine. May we be good stewards of our natural environment. We ask that you be with the prisoners of our jail, those under the care of the sheriff and this court, those who can't experience the beauty of the Ozarks, who are prohibited from feeling the warmth of the sun's rays, from enjoying a sustaining breath of fresh air, from visiting face-to-face with family or friends, or ever tasting a warm, health-giving meal. Keep us mindful of the Gospel writer Matthew's caution that the way we treat the least among us is the way we are treating the Christ. And that whenever we deny proper food to the hungry, visitors to the prisoner, and welcome to the stranger, we have also denied Christ. Forgive us, we pray. Amen."

In my May prayer, I prayed for the newly elected sheriff: "Gracious and Holy One, We are thankful for the opportunity to elect public officials. May those we have elected embrace their sacred duty to be good stewards of our natural environment, protecting the resources you have given us. May those we have elected remember that they have been chosen to represent the interests of all, not just the powerful, the wealthy, and the outspoken. We ask that you instill in the sheriff-elect and the newly elected Quorum Court members a sense of compassion for the poor, the marginalized, and those without advantage. Again we ask that you keep us mindful of the Gospel writer Matthew's admonition that the way we treat the least among us is the way we are treating the Christ. And that whenever we deny proper food to the hungry, visitors to the prisoner, and welcome to the stranger, we have also denied Jesus. Forgive our arrogance and false pride. Grant us humility. In the name of all that is Holy and Just and True, Amen."

The meeting place for the Quorum Court looks like a sparsely attended country church. Seven or eight oak pews are arranged in a row with a solid lectern placed at the head of the pews. However, instead of facing the seated congregants, as in every church I've seen, the lectern is positioned so that the speaker's back is toward the congregation. The speaker faces the elevated, horseshoe-shaped bench around which the members of the court will be seated.

Later that year, I signed up to pray again. Entering the courtroom, I was aware of being noticed, but I was not greeted. Someone was already seated at the end of each pew and no one seemed receptive to the prospect of me sitting beside them, so I continued walking to the empty front pew and took a seat. The Quorum Court members, their clerk, and their attorney, greeted one another as they filtered in. Like the seated assembly, they ignored me.

Sheriff Ferguson, with his Stetson hat in hand, entered through the same door as the judges and filed past me, avoiding my deliberate attempt at eye contact. After the lone female and eleven male judges settled in their places, the presiding judge gaveled the meeting to order and the role was called. The entire assembly stood with right hands on hearts as a full-voiced Pledge of Allegiance was recited. The presider, now seated, leaned toward his microphone and said, "Reverend Roger Joslin, pastor of Radiant Life Church, will lead us in prayer."

I stood and walked the few short steps to the lectern and corrected him: "I'm actually with All Saints' Episcopal Church, here in Bentonville."

"I'm only reading what it says here on this paper," the judge countered.

"Despite what the paper says, I'm from All Saints," I replied and paused a moment before looking around the already hostile room and then requested, "Let us pray."

Heads bowed in reluctant obedience and I offered this prayer:

"Gracious God, we are grateful for your presence with us this evening. We offer you thanks for the rain and the sunshine, the abundance of natural resources surrounding us, and for the beauty of the Ozarks. May we be reminded that we are stewards of that environment and are responsible for the care of your creation. We ask for forgiveness for our role in the creation of the hellish place that is the Benton County jail. . . ."

At this moment, I heard grumbling from the back pew, something like, "That SOB, get out of my way, I've gotta get out of here."

As the door squeaked open and slammed shut, I continued: "And we pray that, in the New Year, under new leadership, the jail may instead become a place of rehabilitation and redemption. May this elected body remember that they are representatives of all residents in the county, the rich and the poor, the powerful and the powerless. And may their decisions reflect your desire for justice, fairness, and compassion. We ask these things in the name of all that is holy and good. Amen."

At the end of a prayer, I'm accustomed to hearing a hearty "Amen" voiced in unison from the All Saints' congregation. At the end of this prayer, only a few mumbled as scattered voices violated the silence in the courtroom. I turned toward the assembly and this time every eye caught mine. Passing the last pew, I turned to the sole smiling face and asked, "Where's the sheriff?"

"He left," she replied, "Do you want to take the back way out?"

"Not hardly," I said, "I was hoping to meet up with him." I took the stairs from the third floor courtroom down to the lobby, expecting to find the sheriff waiting. Instead, one of his young deputies sat idly at the reception desk. "Goodnight," I offered.

"Goodnight, sir," the deputy replied.

CHAPTER 13

Searching for Walmart's Soul

No one can serve two masters; for a slave
will either hate the one and love the other,
or be devoted to the one and despise the
other. You cannot serve God and wealth.

—Matthew 6:24

A s a church planter, my job is to work with fellow spiritual seekers in Benton County to create a new Episcopal church. My days are spent finding people. Just as Phillip found Nathanael and told him about Jesus, I tell people about this new band of Jesus's followers that is forming in Bentonville. It is a truly exciting endeavor. Creating a Christian community in the shadow of what is perhaps the world's most powerful corporation presents opportunities and challenges like no other church plant. But I came to realize, over the first few months here, that it is the angels among us that will show us the way. What I'm really doing is attending to the presence of God's messengers. I am in the enviable position of witnessing the procession of angels as they ascend and descend a ladder to heaven.

I'm learning that the primary task of church planting in the shadow of an empire isn't merely to find a piece of earth and build a church, but to recognize those places where heaven and earth collide. I know that the progressive and fair-minded citizens of places outside of Benton County sometimes tend to look at the goings-on in Bentonville with a bit of skepticism. They are sometimes tempted to ask, in the way that Nathanael did when observing that Jesus came from the lowly-regarded village of Nazareth, "Can anything good come out of Bentonville?"

And just as an answer came to Jacob as he woke from his troubled sleep amid the hard stones on the plains between Beer-sheba and Haran, I have to proclaim as well, "Surely the Lord is in this place—and I did not know it." And just as Jacob's revelation was accompanied by the presence of ascending and descending angels, so has my vision of what a church would be like in Bentonville also been illuminated by the vertical passage of angelic hosts.

Angels, in our midst, proclaiming of Bentonville as Jacob did of the land that was to become Israel: "How awesome is this place! This is none other than the house of God, and this is the gate of heaven." These are the angels among us who, by their presence, point the way to Christ. However, if I may be permitted to take this rather high-flying notion of angels down a notch once more, let's understand that strength, light, healing, and messages from God are also provided by angels absent wings, that is, by the angels who live, work, and walk among the people of All Saints' and among this community of Bentonville. It is a love for Christ that enables the people of All Saints' to recognize, empower, and create angels in our midst.

Racing Hearts

During my first week living in Bentonville, I went to Walmart to buy some black dye in order to dye my brown shoes. Since my ordination, I always wear black clerical clothing and my many brown shoes no longer match. I hoped this would work since I did not want to spend the money on new shoes and I long to be able to easily slip off my Merrill's. At the register I chatted with the checker.

"How are you today?"

"Good, now that I'm about to go home."

"Long day?"

"Nine hours."

"All on your feet, here at the check-out stand?"

"We get breaks, but I'm tired."

The checker was quite overweight and I imagined how swollen and tired her feet and legs must be. However, she remained cheerful and smiled freely, exposing the single visible tooth remaining in her mouth: one upper incisor that gave her the unfortunate appearance of a chipmunk.

"Are the wages good?" I asked.

In response, she just tilted her head to the side and grimaced slightly and with her smile gone, hummed a non-committal tune.

"Maybe you need a union."

"We got an open-door policy. We got an open-door policy," she blurted out as quickly as her now constricted voice could emerge from her near-empty mouth. "We can talk to the management anytime we want. If we have any problem, we can talk to them. And I've done it. You work for a union?"

"No," I answered, "but my father was a union man."

"We got an open-door policy. . . thank you sir."

I felt as if I had thrown this poor woman into near panic. She had been trained well. I could imagine a training session in which anyone who was approached by a union organizer was instructed to inform them of their "open-door" policy. I also imagined that they were also instructed to inform their supervisor if they were approached. I strangely felt that here at Walmart Store 100, directly across the street from the headquarters of the most powerful corporation in the world, I had threatened the empire. My heart raced as rapidly as the heart of the toothless cashier.

Prophets

Perhaps it is not always the case that the prophet garners no respect in his hometown. My experience with small towns is that the man or woman who leaves home and comes back with some measure of success is usually celebrated. The town often feels pride in the accomplishments of the conquering hero, whether they be a sports figure, politician, or successful businessperson. You don't have to look much farther than Sam Walton, a name spoken in hushed tones in Benton County, to know that the successful hometown boy can be the recipient of unlimited honor and accolades. I'm inclined to think that it's not so much whether the prophet is from out of town, or does his prophesying in his native land, that determines how the prophetic words are received. I suggest that it is the nature of the prophet's message that really determines the honor accorded to the messenger.

In the end, it's not really so important whether the prophet is a hometown boy or an expert from out of town with a briefcase. Jesus was chased out of Nazareth, not because he was a local prophet, but because he offended the powers that be. Sam Walton remains a hero in Bentonville because of his strong entrepreneurial spirit, his lack of pretension, and his honest dealings with others, but he never seriously challenged the dominant culture's conception of how we are to live in the world. Jesus does.

The Consolation of Riches

One afternoon, I was driving south on Moberly Lane in Bentonville while holding in the back of my mind, as I often do, a passage from scripture. It's the reading that holds in stark contrast the blessing

Jesus extended toward the poor, the hungry, and the weeping with the woe that Jesus bestows on the rich, the full, and the laughing. In that frame of mind, I couldn't help noticing that on my right was a construction project with a sign that proudly boasted: Coming Soon, Northwest Arkansas Cadillac. I drove a little further down the road and saw another building under construction with a sign that read: Coming Soon, Northwest Arkansas Mercedes-Benz. And before I had time to fully process the implications of building, not one, but two luxury automobile dealerships during recovery from a severe economic recession, I passed a third building with a sign that proclaimed: Coming Soon, Northwest Arkansas BMW.

Recall the small weathered signs that are still occasionally seen behind barbed wire fences along country roads in Arkansas and throughout the South. For instance, signs printed with bold letters that read "John 3:16" or "Jesus saves." I was tempted to go out after dark one evening and add a similar sign in the shadow of this Trinitarian tribute to fine motoring. My sign would quote Luke: "But woe to you who are rich, for you have received your consolation" (Luke 6:24). Now, I will admit, a sweet little convertible BMW, with an infinitely adjustable leather seat and an engine that accelerates like a rocket is not a bad consolation prize; just thinking about it makes me want to sign up for a test drive.

Deep down, we know that the blessing of wealth isn't all it's cracked up to be. Rich and poor alike can live lives of deep anguish and pain. Jesus knew this as well. In the version of the Beatitudes that is most commonly quoted, which is from Matthew's "Sermon on the Mount," Jesus is heard saying, not just "blessed are you who are poor" (Luke 6:24), but "blessed are the poor in spirit" (Matt. 5:3). In that sermon, Jesus recognizes that poverty can just as easily be an affliction of the soul as an affliction of the pocketbook. However, in Luke's Gospel we are told that "Jesus stood on a level place" (Luke 6:17). This wasn't the Sermon on the Mount, where Jesus spoke from a lofty, spiritual summit. This message, known as the "Sermon on the Plain," was an occasion where a fully grounded Jesus was speaking eye-to-eye with the common people. It doesn't take an exhaustive knowledge of the Gospels to recognize that the economically poor occupy a special place in Jesus's heart. These are the recipients of a unique blessing and are specifically offered citizenship in the kingdom of God. But where does that leave those of us who are rich? By the world's standards, the rich includes most of us in this country. If we profess to follow the example and teachings of Jesus, we must recognize that we have already been blessed. In the manner of Christ, we must extend our blessings to the weeping, the hungry, and the poor.

I think that trip down Moberly Lane had the immense impact on me that it did because I had just returned from a meeting with a young lady named Leticia. Leticia, a student at the Northwest Arkansas Community College, wishes to become a broadcast journalist and is among the brightest students in her class. She is smart, articulate, energetic, and pretty. She has a smile that shows even through her tears. She is the kind of student that would normally be offered scholarships to the finest colleges in the land. Instead, although her family is poor, she is required to pay many times the usual cost of tuition. She is at an age when the average Benton County student has her own car, or at least a family car to borrow. Leticia rode to see me on her bicycle because she doesn't have a driver's license. Leticia is well read, politically aware, but isn't permitted to vote. She is of an age when most kids are rather carefree, optimistic about what the future holds, and boldly testing their potential. However, she is compelled to always stay vigilant, aware that at any moment, she could be apprehended and deported to a land that she does not know.

Leticia was brought to this country from Mexico by her parents when she was three years old. She has never visited the land of her origin. She is a model member of society, except that she is not a citizen. In addition to supporting herself within a shadow economy that doesn't permit her to work legally, she bravely advocates on behalf of the Dream Act. The Dream Act would grant the best and brightest of a generation a way to move out of the poverty that comes from living in the shadows, engage in the blessings that we take for granted, and in return, bless us.

Specifically, the Dream Act would give undocumented young people who arrived in the U.S. as minors and graduate from US high schools the opportunity to earn permanent residency, if they complete a term of service in the military or graduate from college. Unfortunately, lawmakers from all sides of the political spectrum have so far lacked the courage to offer their blessing to the creation of a legal path for immigration for even for our most deserving potential citizens.

In Luke's Gospel, Jesus tells us that God wants us to bless the hated, the excluded, and the reviled. This is a portrait that looks a lot like the undocumented immigrant. Woe unto those who stand in the way of God's desire to bless. While there is hope for the rich, I don't know if it is the news that we want to hear. The poor are empty and hungry; God's love flows easily into such emptiness. Those of us who are rich are prone to be full, satisfied, and complacent; there is not a lot of room left for God to get inside. A place has to be created for God to dwell. There may be other ways, but the simplest path to salvation for the rich is to give wealth away. The poor are easily blessed because their poverty compels them to rely on God. We, the rich, are far more prone to rely on ourselves.

In the end, no matter whether you drive a luxury car or ride a bicycle, you are loved, fully enclosed in the circle of God's compassion. Jesus, in plain language, is asking those of us who call ourselves his followers, to heed his example and offer our blessing to those that Jesus blessed. This includes the poor, the hungry, the weeping, the hated, the excluded, and the reviled. And if we are seeking a deeper connection with God we are called to do likewise.

Jerusalem Was a Company Town

Upton Sinclair wrote, "It is difficult to get a man to understand something when his salary depends on his not understanding it." All Saints' is located in the quintessential company town. Almost every parishioner works for Walmart, for a Walmart vendor, or for a company or institution that provides goods or services to those in the corporate network. All Saints' has a thriving and healthy congregation because of Walmart's presence.

Bentonville is a city with rather low unemployment, decent schools, parks and trails, a vibrant downtown, and even a major art museum. Certainly, this is all because of Walmart. Indeed, Bentonville is a good place to live. But these assets can be seductive and lead us to complacency. Prosperity can tempt us to lose our prophetic spirit.

Jesus was nurtured, educated, and sustained by the temple. The temple was the center of religion, culture, and identity. The temple was at the heart of what it meant to be Jewish. Jerusalem was a company town. Nonetheless, Jesus was unwilling to turn a blind eye to practices that violated sacred principles. He raged against unethical behavior within the institution that was at the heart of his universe.

I wonder if progressive church plants like All Saints' are willing to do the same. No matter where a church is planted, are we willing to turn a critical eye toward business practices that violate norms of justice and compassion? Are we willing to speak up when a culture with a strong work ethic, which is a good thing, exceeds reasonable expectations and expects an employee to spend excessive hours away from family and life-giving activities? Do we keep silent when an employer's labor practices make it impossible for workers to organize and engage in collective bargaining so they can lay claim to workers rights and to a living wage? Do we speak up when a company uses the advantage of its bargaining power to push suppliers beyond what is reasonable and fair? Are we willing to indirectly profit from the labor of Chinese peasants working very long hours, for very low wages, far from their families?

It's not that the pursuit of everyday low prices is a harmful idea; it's actually very noble. But when people suffer because of the low wages required to keep the prices low and the profits high, then the prophetic imagination is called to find its voice. We can share the values of an institution but still be critical of it. In fact, if the tradition of the prophets and the legacy of the Christ is to be our guide, then we are called to do just that. We worship a God who is of us, with us, and for us. But we must also recognize that the voices of God's prophets might also speak against us. May we be attuned to those voices as well.

Entrepreneurial Spirit

I shared lunch with a brilliant and compassionate young entrepreneur. After serving time in the trenches of Walmart's information technology division, Austin and his business partner, Mark, launched their own firm, developing software that will enable their clients to visualize and manipulate vast amounts of data, bringing to life information that would, for most users, remain dense and indecipherable. The same sense of vitality that Austin brings to his work, he also brings to his spiritual quest by reacting against the jargon of Christianity, rejecting the narrowness of his childhood faith, and searching for a new way to understand the nature of God.

As the co-owner of a business startup, Austin brings to the enterprise the skills to succeed, but his strong sense of morality and concern for the well-being of his employees and the world at large could put him at a competitive disadvantage in a business climate where unfettered capitalism is the prevalent practice. Even though his firm is small and barely in the black, 20 percent of the profits are given away, currently to a girls' hotel in Uganda. Austin is now struggling with how to provide benefits to his full-time employees, particularly health insurance. He was most dismayed when a representative from a major health insurance company advised him against hiring any employees with existing illnesses and to find a way to fire those who get sick. And now finding himself wearing the boss's hat, Austin is seeking ways to respect the rights of his employees, to enable them to bring life to their own imaginative impulses, while at the same time create a common, shared vision of the company's goals.

Austin's imagination isn't bound by a narrow concern for the success of his own small enterprise. Looking around him, Austin is aware of the extraordinarily unique opportunity that exists here in Benton County. There is probably not another city on the planet where such a large collection of the representatives of major American corporations has assembled and are actively engaged in doing business in one location. It would be a big deal if the number of corporations that have offices in Benton County were collected in New York City or Chicago. However, for those thousands of companies to have decision-makers gathered in a rural Arkansas county where daily interaction is possible, an unprecedented opportunity is presented for us to make the world a better place.

For example, I'm fairly certain that neither Walmart, Proctor & Gamble, PepsiCo, nor Kraft really want to be in the business of providing health insurance for their employees. However, the irrational system of employer provided insurance is the arrangement under which these companies now reluctantly operate. Imagine how the meeting of the minds of Bentonville executives, intent on changing the system, could find creative avenues for providing health care for everyone who needs it. Or imagine if all these companies that do business with Walmart could recognize that climate change is a threat to us all and then bring the power of their collective imagination to finding ways to reduce their carbon footprint.

Instead of simply railing against government regulation, this little corner of Northwest Arkansas could become the harbinger of a different way of doing business. These companies came to Bentonville in order to do business with Walmart. However, the potential for this unique gathering of creative minds and collective energy to change the face of contemporary capitalism is unprecedented. If we can wake up to that realization, then the time we have spent here together will have been far more fruitful than a simple-minded quest to improve the bottom line.

There is a refreshing naiveté in Austin's approach to business. He recognizes that raw capitalism, driven only by a concern for profits, runs counter to his desire to live a Christian, moral life. Thus, he seeks an alternative way. Perhaps it is time to listen to the unjaded voices of the young.

Alignment of Interests

One Sunday, I had a conversation with a woman who is on the outer circle of All Saints' membership. She is among those people who rarely attend, but still calls All Saints' home and considers me to be her priest. She and her husband are close friends of the Walton family. As she explained to me once: "The Waltons are Presbyterians and will always remain so. But they are progressive in their thinking and I have talked with them about our church. They are very interested in the idea of our building an open-minded church. They also have an interest in the redevelopment of downtown and in our plan to build a church in the neighborhood near the Crystal Bridges Museum of American Art. I think they might be supportive in some way. How? I'm not exactly sure. We are close friends and I wouldn't ever do anything to take advantage of that friendship, but we should think of a way of keeping them in the loop concerning what we are doing."

My own take on a potential Walton involvement is that Walmart is very interested in having Bentonville perceived as an international and forward-thinking community. In much the same way that they desire to be perceived as a corporation that is sensitive to the environment, the desire to be perceived in that way can mean that they actually make changes in policy and practices that result in them moving in the direction of being a sustainable company. They can't operate entirely by illusion, so they want to attract people into leadership roles at Walmart from around the globe. It is a great selling point if they can say to a potential executive from India, "You will find a Hindu temple where you can worship and gather with other Hindus in Bentonville," or to a Muslim from Indonesia, "We have a mosque where you can pray." It's part of the package of offering good schools, running and biking trails, shopping, and even an art museum that is comparable to the Getty.

The Conscience of the Corporation

The world watched in horror as the decomposing bodies of more than eight hundred people were pulled from the rubble of a charred and collapsed garment factory in Bangladesh. Most of the workers who toiled daily and then died inside the over-crowded eight-story building earned little more than the national minimum wage of $38 a month.

As dreadful as the incident is, the oceans, as well as the cultural and economic differences that separate America from a remote factory in Bangladesh, allow us to ignore the tragedy. Yet, the fact that Bangladesh exports $20 billion a year in garments to the US and Europe means that it is quite possible that both you and I, at this very moment, are wearing a T-shirt or other article of clothing that was stitched and sewn by the hands of a person crushed beneath the tumbling walls of a slipshod manufacturing plant. We are connected with the young men and women in that Bangladeshi factory and with all those who work in factories around the world. We are all God's children.

We wear the clothes, sit on the chairs, use the electronics, and allow our children to play with toys that are fabricated by the hands of people who have the same right to decent standards of living, health, and safety that we expect. As American consumers who occupy the same shrinking planet as workers in the developing world, we have a responsibility to consider the well-being of those who make the things we want and need.

What can we do? For starters, we can ask questions in order to learn something about the origin of the products we buy, we can demand that retailers, distributors, importers, and manufacturers have some knowledge about the source of the items we wear and use, and we can find out about the working conditions and the environmental impact of producing the things we purchase. As consumers, we are accustomed to making choices based on price, quality, and style. Is it too much for us to also consider the welfare of those who make the items we buy? Or to consider what effect our purchases have on the air we breathe and the climate we inhabit? These are important questions that may be asked and choices that can be made by any thoughtful consumer or any person whose sense of justice and morality compels them to look beyond the limits of our nation's borders. These are the economic choices available to any American.

There are a lot of different occupations represented at All Saints': carpenters, bakers, teachers, doctors, counselors, salespersons, architects, chicken processors, lawyers, nurses, clerks, police officers, bankers, accountants, artists, horticulturalists, inn keepers, writers, social workers, and a whole host of folks with titles like "Senior Manager Global Talent Insights" or "Manager Systems International Compliance."

Thomas Carlisle once wrote, "Blessed is the man who has found his work; let him ask no other blessedness." The truth in that statement compels me to probe more deeply into the true nature of the work we are called to do. The residents of Northwest Arkansas are in a unique position to do more than the average American could even dream of doing. As home to the world's largest retailer, as well as the place where thousands of US based corporations have chosen to locate key offices, Bentonville is in a position to have an effect on business, labor, and environmental policy far beyond the Ozarks. The policies developed by Walmart, their vendors, and allied corporations have the potential to positively impact wages and working conditions, environmental policy, health care, child labor practices, and a host of other quality of life issues that are beyond the reach of humanitarian organizations and governmental entities.

While a corporation cannot be expected to have a conscience, the people who work for and with corporations do. We are called by God to use the means available to us to make the world a better place. The people of Northwest Arkansas have the means not simply to engage in charity, but to actually change the face of the planet. Where in the world could a person share a cup of coffee with a man or woman who purchases millions of dollars worth of shoes or toys and is in a position to ask a factory owner in China how their employees are treated? Where on the planet could a person have a conversation with a neighbor who can choose to buy goods from a company with factories that pollute or one with those that don't? I ask my parishioners to live into the opportunity that God has presented to them, not simply to help avoid tragedies like those in Bangladesh, but to touch the lives of all those around the world with whom many of them engage in commerce, even if it is from a distance of ten thousand miles. Indeed, we are all in a distinctive position to make the world a better place.

Alice

Alice had taken her usual place beside the unevenly plastered north wall of the yoga studio, a choice spot for anyone seeking a slight respite from the room's hotter central core or for someone seeking the security of a cool wall to lean on in a balance pose. We sometimes chatted about our mutual connection to the Cross Plains region of Texas where my mother and her quarter horses reside, our physical ailments, or the exhibits at the museum she funded, Crystal Bridges Museum of American Art. It seems slightly ridiculous to say that life has not always been easy for one of the wealthiest women in the United States, but it's true. Alice has lived as close to the wild side as is possible for a little girl who grew up in small-town Bentonville.

I had been more regular in my attendance at the 9:00 a.m. class because I hoped that an opportunity would present itself to show Alice the land that had been purchased for the new church building. If Alice was in town, she often attended the morning class. If my schedule wasn't too heavy, I would attend it as well.

A series of DWIs and a few car wrecks that left one pedestrian killed had all taken an emotional and physical toll on Alice. I recognized the pain in her misshapen feet. Foot ailments can be both the physical source for much pain and, at the same time, the vessel for emotional pain. Clearly in discomfort, Alice would move through the poses with perhaps too much determination. The yoga teacher's instructions to "relax through the pose" often go unheeded by Alice. Possessing her ambitious father's grit, she does not allow limitations to prevent her from getting a pose "right."

My wife, Cindee, wasn't teaching the class that Monday morning, but knowing of my desire to find an opportune moment to connect with Alice, she usually monitored attendance at the class from her computer at home. Discovering that Alice was in class, Cindee instinctively prayed that something would transpire between us. Poojah, the teacher from Southern India, began to lead the class through a series of poses. It is ideally the goal, and always a challenge, to remain fully present to the immediate during a yoga class. This day it proved to be a complete impossibility for me.

Just the day before, All Saints' celebrated the Day of Pentecost by holding Sunday morning worship services under a large tent on the church building site. We have multiple services each week in English and Spanish and our combined congregation has now grown too large for us to meet together in the nave of Christ the King Church. Meeting on our newly purchased land also provided the opportunity for the parishioners to imagine what it would be like to hold services on the site. The conceptual design of the permanent building was nearing completion and the architect had constructed a scale model of the proposed church building. Since we had no place to safely store the model, we intended to return it to the architect in Fayetteville later in the day. After the worship service, the model was carried back to Christ the King Church and set up temporarily in the parish hall.

Moving through a *chaturanga* pose, I realized that the perfect moment had arrived to show Alice the church design. Usually my heart rate slows down during a yoga class, but this morning it raced at the prospect of revealing the design to her. I carefully rehearsed what I would say to Alice at the end of class, planning how I could present the offer to her as an opportunity rather than as a coercion. Alice often left class before it had completely ended. As the teacher would instruct the class to move into savasana, or corpse pose, Alice would often rise and quietly roll up her mat and ease out the door. I sometimes wondered if it was the urgency of a meeting that compelled her to leave or a reluctance to allow herself the exquisitely challenging pleasure of lying in perfect, thoughtless, stillness.

From the corner of my eye, I could see that Alice had stayed on the mat throughout *savasana*. As she rolled up her mat, a perky young woman approached Alice, introduced herself, and thanked her for bringing Crystal Bridges to Bentonville. Alice kindly acknowledged her thanks and headed for the door. As she passed by my mat, I said, "Alice, I have something I think you would like to see."

"What's that, Roger?" she asked. I was surprised, albeit pleasantly, that she had remembered my name.

"I think you know that Marlon Blackwell is designing a church for us."

"Yes, I've heard that," she responded.

"Well, we had a church service on our land yesterday and we had the model that Marlon's team set up there. We're going to take it back to the architect's office this afternoon, but right now it's in the parish hall at Christ the King Church, where we meet. Would you like to see it?"

"Yes, I would. Very much."

When we walked from the studio into the foyer, I could see that Poojah was on the phone. I learned later that during the class Cindee had received a phone call from Alice's assistant, saying that it was very important that she speak with Alice as soon as possible. Cindee explained that there wasn't a phone inside the studio and that it wasn't possible for her to interrupt the class. Cindee agreed to call the studio as soon as class had ended and to relay the message to Alice. As Alice and I chatted, I could hear Poojah on the line. "Yes, she is still here. She is talking with Roger about the church."

"Oh, I see," Cindee replied, knowing how critical this conversation might be. "Never mind; that's okay. Don't interrupt them," Cindee said, while she hung up the phone.

"We can walk. The church is just a couple of blocks away. Or take my truck, if you like," I offered.

"That's okay, I've got my little buggy here. I know where the church is, I'll meet you there." Alice had driven to the yoga studio in the glorified golf cart used to ferry dignitaries and persons who are disabled around the grounds of Crystal Bridges and parked it in front in a non-designated parking spot. Arriving ahead of Alice, I waited in the church parking lot. Alice was on her cell phone when she cruised into the empty parking lot. I could overhear her saying, "Yes, I think $16 million would be okay. We're already strong in . . . And I'd like to add to the collection. Yeah go ahead and make the offer."

I had read how many of the museum's acquisitions were made while Alice sat atop a quarter horse on her ranch in Texas. Now, I had just witnessed firsthand how millions of dollars could be spent more casually than when I order salmon for lunch. I led Alice into the parish hall to the model and removed the Plexiglas cover so that it could be more easily seen. "Oooh. . . it's beautiful," Alice said, as she looked the model over.

"You like it?" I asked.

"Very much, very much," she replied.

I had listened to the architect explain the design dozens of times and was able to similarly describe the progression of the space, how one moves from the lower, wide, and welcoming entryway, through an interior garden, into the narthex, passing through a ribbon of light, into the nave with its undulating ceiling and veiled light, and finally into a high-ceilinged small chapel at the apex of the triangular-shaped building. "It's movement," I explained, "toward the sacred, from the ordinary into the transcendent." I explained in greater detail, "The idea is for people to move from the entrance, the wide front porch, through not one red door, as is typical for Episcopal churches, but through twelve open red doors, that welcome them into the garden, or garth. In the garth will be sculpture, perhaps a fountain, and spaces for people to gather for liturgical events or just to be together. From the garden they will move into the narthex, passing through a ribbon of light streaming from above and then into the nave. The nave has a high, faceted wooden ceiling. The exterior of the nave is composed of perforated metal panels that allow light to pass through. Then there is a clear glass surface, with sheer, gauze-like curtains that create a shroud-like atmosphere within the worship space. At the north end of the nave is a small chapel. It is designed to be simple, with whitewashed plaster walls and benches, perhaps reminiscent of the interior of a colonial church in Latin America. As one moves from porch, to garden, to narthex, to nave, to chapel, and finally to the apex of the triangle, there is movement through degrees of holiness, through spaces that seem more and more removed from the world, with a sense of movement toward the sacred."

"I get it. It's fabulous," Alice exclaimed. "This is exactly what I wanted to happen. I hoped that after Crystal Bridges was built that the quality of architecture in Bentonville would be different. This is exactly what I had hoped."

"I'm so glad you like it. Marlon is a very talented designer," I added.

"I think he is a genius. He is the Fay Jones of his generation," Alice remarked. Fay Jones is the most renowned architect Arkansas has ever seen. He was a student of Frank Lloyd Wright and is most noted for designing Thorncrown Chapel in Eureka Springs. It is indeed high praise in Arkansas to be compared to Fay Jones.

At that moment, I was very tempted to ask Alice if she could help us build the church. It seemed an opportune moment. However, Bishop Benfield had made it very clear to me that, even if the opportunity presented itself, he should be the one to ask. I wasn't so certain that this was the wisest approach. Alice strikes me as a very direct, straight shooter. A more formal "asking" might be best, but

I left our meeting hoping I hadn't allowed an opportunity to pass by. Nevertheless, important groundwork had been laid.

A few weeks later, after another yoga class with Alice, I sat on the bench in the waiting room putting on my shoes. Alice sat down beside me and asked, "How is the church coming along?"

I answered her saying, "Nicely. We have just completed the geo-tech drilling that is required for a determination of the foundation requirements for the structure."

"How much is the church going to cost?" she inquired.

"Well, that's what we are trying to determine now. The construction manager is in the process of putting together a more accurate estimate of the cost. However, the architects original estimates were about five or six million."

"I see. And how much are the architect's fees?"

"They are based on the cost of construction." "About 15 percent?" Alice asked.

"Yes, something like that."

The next week, I received a call from the architect who let me know that he and his family had been given a tour of an exhibit by Alice. Along the way they talked about the church. Marlon explained that, at one point, Alice stopped the tour, turned to him and said, "I want to see this church built." In Bentonville, when a member of the Walton family wants something done, it generally gets done.

CHAPTER 14

Creating Sacred Space

Then he said, "Come no closer! Remove
the sandals from your feet, for the place on
which you are standing is holy ground."

—Exodus 3:5

John Donahue, the Irish poet, priest, and philosopher, speaks
of the sense of mystery and transcendence that emerges from
the intersection of nature, the body, and the senses, by suggesting, "God is beauty." Donahue speaks of beauty not simply
as that which is glamorous, pretty, or appealing, but that which
transforms us and moves us closer to the truth about who we
are. As Donahue says, beauty contains "an emerging fullness,
a greater sense of grace and elegance, a deeper sense of depth,
and also a kind of homecoming for the enriched memory of your
unfolding life."

We are a people of pilgrimage, a people who are sharing a journey and seeking that day of homecoming. Imagine a Sunday when a young child who is an All Saints' parishioner will remove the processional cross from its stand by the altar. Other acolytes, wearing crisp clean albs, will hold their torches, as another grasps the Gospel book. Together, they will lift their cross, torches, and Gospel book high and they will walk, not just to the back of the nave at Christ the King Church, but out the front doors and onto the street. And we, the people of All Saints', the people of Todos los Santos, will follow them. We will march together, hundreds of us, up Central Avenue to the Bentonville Square. Along the way, we will pray, sing, and read Holy Scripture, giving thanks to God for accompanying us on the journey. And we will turn left onto Main Street and process with trumpets blaring toward our new home. With the cross lifted high, we will march to the end of Main Street and walk onto sacred ground.

Every member of All Saints' is already engaged in the act of creating sacred space, even those who never say a word about paint color or express a thought about foundations or landscape. A person's presence, their sense of mindfulness, and their consideration for the well-being of others, shapes the environment around them and touches the hearts and minds of their fellow parishioners. We are all called to marvelous work. *Que son llamados por Dios a obra maravillosa.*

I've been listening to the members of All Saints'. I've been listening to what they have told me about the church they want to build. Some have told me that they want a red door. Others have told me that they want a columbarium. Everyone has told me that they want a place to kneel and pray. And many have told me that they simply want our building to look like a church. What I do promise is a sacred place, a place of remembrance, where we are reminded each time when we step onto the property that we are on holy ground. The building will be known as a place where God resides. While it will not necessarily have soaring towers or magnificent symbols of our religion, the building will be filled with gentle reminders of the transcendent spirit of God. These reminders are as subtle as the crunching sound of crushed granite beneath our feet, the sweet smell of wildflowers lining a path, and the smooth touch of a well-worn door handle.

The best of art and architecture reminds us who we are, teaches us something about ourselves, and tells us who we aspire to be. When we set out to create a sacred space, we are not simply asking God to transform a stony bluff into a "house of God," we are also asking that we be transformed.

All Saints' practices radical hospitality and possesses a welcoming spirit that moves far beyond friendliness or even mere tolerance. We strive for true graciousness and full-hearted acceptance of those who are different from ourselves. And that kind of generous spirit requires that the presence of God be made known to all who enter this church. To ask for God's presence is to ask that God not leave us alone. When we ask for God's presence in a place, we should know what we are asking for. While we might expect comfort, reassurance, and peace, the presence of God can often bring discomfort, challenge, and a push in the direction that we are not sure we want to go.

Recall Jacob's dream in which he wrestled with an angel and climbed a ladder that stretched to heaven. It was a mystical experience that was about more than the nature of Jacob's singular relationship with a personal God. Rather, it was about the formation of a people. The dream occurred in a place where God would visit Jacob again and again, a place where God would rename him Israel and tell him how he would father a nation.

This place, called Bethel, was formed and pruned by the people; the people were pruned and formed by the place. Indeed, both people and place were made holy by the presence of God. God is forming us now, pruning away what is not life giving, and strengthening us for the work of creating a house of God. God's messengers, the angels ascending and descending the ladder to heaven, told Jacob that God would not leave him alone until God had done what he had promised. And on the day when the people of All Saints' walk onto that holy ground at the north end of Main Street, they will declare with Jacob: "How awesome is this place! This is none other than the house of God, and this is the gate of heaven."

Imagine it as a place of remembrance, a place were we intentionally recall that we are to take on the mind of Christ. Imagine church as a place designed to remove the focus from our own needs, ambitions, desires and bring our attention to the well-being, hopes, suffering, and joy of others. The faces and families of the people in any church are a unique collection of people. There are churchgoers who choose to attend a church that best suits their needs. They search for a place with perfectly executed liturgy, a professional choir, acolytes who never make a misstep, and with a multitude of programs for young, old, and everyone in-between. And then there are those who are called to adventure.

Opportunities to participate in great work, to be a part of something truly significant, do not present themselves often in life. Recall from Shakespeare's play the words spoken by King Henry V as he rallied his beleaguered troops to do battle with the waiting French army: "And gentlemen in England now a-bed / Shall think themselves accursed they were not here." In the years to come, the founding generation of All Saints' parishioners will tell stories of their hard work of planting, growing, and building a progressive church in Bentonville to their children and to their children's children. Surely there will be a sense of regret among those who chose to not take part in this thrilling adventure.

An institution, whether it be a church, a company, or a college, carries in its DNA the genius and the pathology of its founding families. Those who have the privilege of creating a church also carry with them an incredible responsibility. The founding families of All Saints' will transmit a way of being, for better or for ill, to the generations that will follow. Established institutions can change, but only with great difficulty. These early members are laying the groundwork for the character, the personality, and the saintliness that will persist far beyond the day in which they are all gone.

The children of the founding families of All Saints' will someday sit on the vestry, serve at the altar, and grow the church far beyond its current limited vision. This next generation will have the current church leadership to thank for creating an atmosphere of love, compassion, and generosity and for building a sacred space where all are welcome and all can touch the transcendent spirit of God Almighty. I invite progressive church planters from every walk of life to partake in God's creative energy and join us in this adventure of creating sacred space.

Visioning

Much time and careful consideration was devoted to the process of selecting an architect to design our sacred space. A large number of architects were considered and the field was eventually narrowed to three. Any of the three would have been acceptable and would have designed a fine building. However, our selection committee was concerned that none of the three had the creative vision to design a structure that reflected the complex vibrancy of our community. Eventually, we interviewed Marlon Blackwell, the chairman of the Department of Architecture at the University of Arkansas, who is also one of the country's most talented contemporary architects. After a few meetings, we were convinced that Mr. Blackwell possessed sufficient creative energy and talent to design our space.

Occurring simultaneously with the architect interview process, we held a series of visioning sessions at All Saints'. The aim of the sessions was to more clearly define who we were as a people of God and to call out our identity so that we could then convey to the architect our conception of what we were about. In order for the architect to design a building for All Saints', he or she had to first understand who we were. And if we are to accurately communicate our corporate character, we had to understand it ourselves.

We gathered representatives from the wide range of constituencies that make up the All Saints' community so that individuals with a shared interest could talk about their collective vision for All Saints'. Representatives from the music program, the altar guild, the hospitality guild, parents and youth, outreach, the vestry, Christian education, and many others, met as an individual interest group to share their thoughts. Each group was asked the following questions:

How would you describe All Saints' today?

How do you imagine All Saints' in the future?

What kind of church building would convey those images of All Saints'?

What do we want a building to say about us?

What will we gain when we build a new building?

What will we lose?

Answers to the questions were recorded on a marker board and compiled across the various groups. The same sort of descriptors came up over and over again to characterize All Saints':

Diverse	Youthful	Challenging
Multicultural	Community-Minded	Accepting
Inclusive	Giving	Inspirational
Spiritual	Fluid	Exploring
Welcoming	Active	Grateful
Progressive	Real	Conscious
Open-Minded	Harmonious	Healthy
Friendly	Sincere	Vibrant
Hospitable	Seeking	Informal
Inviting	Loving	Fun-loving
Comfortable	Caring	Liberal
Eclectic	Intimate	
Bilingual	Radical	

While many expressed an openness to evolve over time, the shared vision of who we would become in the future was firmly grounded in the identity of the present. The challenge we issued to the architect was to design a building that reflected who we were at the time and then would help enable us to become the people of

God that we aspired to be in the future. For example, if we think of ourselves as an open, welcoming, and inclusive community, then we wouldn't want to build a formidable, windowless, fortress-like structure, with an entrance that is hard to find. If we are a congregation that welcomes the poor, the marginalized, and those in need, then the church shouldn't be so opulent and formal that it seems to the outsider to be "a rich person's church." At the same time, if we have an appreciation for the sacred path provided by beauty and holiness, the building should reflect our regard for attention to detail and artfulness. If we profess to care about God's creation, then our church must be attune to the need to keep our footprint on the earth small and respectful of the environment.

In this process of determining what kind of church we will build, we are discovering what kind of people we are, and if we are willing to pay the price of discipleship. At the end of the process, we will have erected a sacred space, a place of beauty, transcendence, and holiness, where for decades to come, people will gather to pray, to learn to love, to serve, and to receive God's grace. But more than erecting a building, the process will transform us into disciples.

A church building ought to be a sanctuary where all that enter experience the living presence of God and know an indwelling of the Spirit. But a church must also become a people who carry the essence of a sacred dwelling within them. Like the snail or the crab that carries their dwelling with them, may we come to know the Divine Breath as the sacred space that resides with us always. Surely then, the words of the Psalmist will become our own: "You are indeed my rock and my fortress; for your name's sake, lead me and guide me" (Ps. 31:3).

Holy Ground

As Thomas Barrie noted in his book *The Sacred In-Between: The Mediating Roles of Architecture,* sacred architecture has the capacity "to connect us with a deeper understanding of ourselves, our relationship with others, and to our place in the cosmos. . . ." I am as eager to see the ground broken for All Saints' as Peter was to start building mountaintop dwellings for Jesus, Moses, and Elijah. But if we allow ourselves to think that we will truly become the church only when we are comfortably ensconced in our magnificent new home, then our time here will be as hollow as the tunnel-riddled haystack of my childhood.

We are called to live in the eternal present and to pitch our tents on holy ground. The holy ground is all around us. As Seymour Glass, the protagonist in J.D. Salinger's novel *Raise High the Roof Beam, Carpenters*, says, ". . . all we do our whole lives is go from one little piece of Holy Ground to the next." The holy ground is wherever we walk. And the holy ground is on our bluff overlooking Tiger Boulevard. We consecrate the ground on which we walk and we make it holy by awakening to the Divine presence that inhabits all of creation.

Foundations

A building does not make the church. All Saints' is much more about building community than putting together brick and mortar. To rush ahead and make plans to build a building before building a congregation that has grown in both size and spiritual depth would be the height of foolishness.

However, an idea has recently taken hold of my imagination. When the time comes, what if we were to construct a worship space that represented to the community at large something of who we are? It would be a place where the doors are open and welcoming and an entryway is designed in a manner that conveys the sense of receptivity and inclusion that we have fostered from our beginnings. It will be a building that hearkens back to our rich Anglican roots, a place where the sacred is conveyed through beauty. It will surely be a sacred space that echoes the psalmist's cry to God, "Be a rock of refuge for me, a strong fortress to save me" (Ps. 31:2), while at the same time being a place whose footprint on the earth's surface is light. I imagine a church that is a model of sensitivity to creation by using God's gifts of wind and sun to provide the power needed to keep the interior warm in the winter, cool in the summer, and always filled with light. I hope for a building designed and oriented in a way that allows it to harmonize with its physical setting, to be as one with the natural world by relying on the insights of the architect Frank Lloyd Wright and his Arkansas protégé Fay Jones. Indeed, this will be a structure that reveals how we value tradition, but conveys a vision of the church of the future. Truly, this is a church worth building. And as thrilling as this prospect is, I know that we are not ready. To begin construction of a church building with inadequate building materials would be building a house on sand.

We have come a long way in a short period of time. But it is critical, at this juncture, to pay close attention to our foundation. We are to hear the words of Jesus and act on them, like a wise man who built his house on rock. We must ensure that progressive church plants like All Saints' are the kinds of places where everyone who enters our doors finds an entry point. It must be foundational that every visitor is made to feel welcome. And then, we must be sure that their spiritual growth is attended to. A church with a solid foundation is a place where the spiritual well-being of young and old alike is nurtured, cared for, instructed, and challenged. If we build without having constructed a foundation that allows all our members to grow into their full potential as Christians, we have built a house on sand.

Those who are part of this creative and thrilling endeavor have a responsibility to pay close attention to the building materials making up the foundation of All Saints'. God entered into the creation process because God had so much love to offer that it couldn't be contained. God needed to be in relationship and we were created to satisfy that need. That need for close relationship permeates our being as well. We must ensure that our foundation is permeated by a love and acceptance of one another. It is vital that prayer, our means of relating to the Divine, becomes part of our being. It is essential that a sense of compassion and justice, for all God's children, motivates us, not just to come here and listen to what it said on Sunday mornings, but to act on the very words of Jesus. Above all, church must be the kind of place that allows all who enter to live into who they are called to be. Any institution that doesn't provide a way for its members to become all that God intended them to be, to realize who they really are, and to find their potential as human beings is wasting time and lives.

In speaking of this imagined house built on a solid foundation, Jesus says, "The rain fell, the floods came, and the winds blew and beat on that house, but it did not fall, because it had been founded on rock" (Matt. 7:25). My prayer is that faithful, open-minded Christians everywhere will pay close attention to the kind of houses they are building. May we act to ensure that when our children's children are members of our churches and when the rains fall, the floods come, and the winds blow and beat against the houses we have built, that they will not fall. Indeed, our houses will never fall because they are founded on the rock of our salvation, which is an irresistible outpouring of Divine Love.

Location

Since my first day in Bentonville, I have had my eyes open for a proper church site location, a piece of fertile land where we might someday scatter seed. Bentonville sits in a large valley on the edges of the hills and mountains of the Ozarks. The land in the valley was once more fertile; cotton, corn, and orchards were the primary source of income before truckers, chickens, and Walmart brought cash. Consequently, most of the available land looks like the discarded and depleted cotton fields they once were. It's land that is ideal for building yet another strip shopping mall and characterless subdivision, both of which abound in Bentonville and the adjacent town of Centerton. Bentonville's growth has followed the path of least resistance, moving primarily in the direction of cheap, flat, easily conquered real estate. It is as if developers absorbed the Walmart mentality and used the same criteria for determining home and business sites that Walmart uses across the country.

The importance of place, the role that having "a sense of place" plays in the formation of community, can't be denied. A church's location is just as important as its design. The particular piece of God's earth that I discovered is at the end of Main Street, one mile north of the Bentonville Square. It is perched on the edge of a bluff, overlooking a verdant valley. A church built on this parcel of land would be visible from both Northwest A Street and the new extension of Tiger Boulevard. Crystal Bridges Museum is within walking distance and the property is easily accessible from every direction via the roads, sidewalks, and trails that network throughout the surrounding area. More importantly, a church planted in this spot would serve as a bridge between two neighborhoods, one lower income and one more affluent, thereby putting the church in direct contact with those in need and with those who have the resources to further God's work in the world.

After determining the site's potential, I understood how suited it would be for the mission of All Saints'. Included within the property is a small parcel of land that is adjacent to the site, but across the street. The land is down a steep descent that follows into a ravine and leads to the gentle valley below, where the deer seek coolness at midday, where the traffic noise is replaced by the sound of falling water, where a creek meanders through a tiny meadow, and where the sense of God's holy presence abounds. It's a natural contemplative garden, a place of prayer, of stillness, and of refuge from the strident aims of the world.

The two levels of the site are illustrative of the nature of the Christian life lived fully, a life that has room for both action and contemplation. A place above to stir our collective imagination, foster community, educate our children, practice our faith, and to launch us into the world. A level below where we can simply be, a holy place to rest in God's peace and allow the seeds we've planted to sprout and grow. Searching for the location of a church is a physical underscoring of the gospel message. We are called to plant the seeds of the kingdom. If the plant grows "first the stalk, then the head, then the full grain in the head" (Mark 4:28), it will be accomplished in God's time and by God's hand. As we watch the growth, we will shake our heads in wonder and amazement.

Formed by Architecture

We are in the process of more clearly establishing our identity as a church that will serve the people of Bentonville and those in the surrounding areas for many years to come. It is important that we do this as we think about the kind of structure we will build on our land. Ultimately, the church structure should announce something about who and what a church is. For generations to come, the building will help form the people who come together in the space. People are formed by the spaces they occupy. Indeed, architecture has an effect on the persons inside. A cluttered, busy space may fill a person with anxiety, while a serene space may calm and move someone toward a sense of contemplation. High vaulted ceilings move toward the transcendent. A sense of artfulness can lead toward an appreciation for beauty. If a people are niggardly in their approach to building, a stinginess beyond frugality could result. If a church fails to be good stewards of its resources and does not design with sustainability in mind, a wasteful attitude might take hold in its future members. The building could be so wasteful of scarce resources that it might eventually become uninhabitable.

An awareness of the future and its effects on our decisions now is a weighty responsibility. We must approach our work knowing that the church must not only meet our needs today and have the flexibility to meet the needs of our children's children, but that it must ultimately form and transform who we are and who future generations will be as part of this Christian community.

Tower Building

I do not recommend this practice, since it seems more like superstition than faith. However, if I were to close my eyes, open my Bible to a random location, blindly stab at a passage, and find that my finger had landed on Luke 14:28–30, I might decide that God works in ways that are even more mysterious than I had once thought. The scripture reads, "For which of you, intending to build a tower, does not first sit down and estimate the cost, to see whether he has enough to complete it? Otherwise, when he has laid a foundation and is not able to finish, all who see it will begin to ridicule him, saying, 'This fellow began to build and was not able to finish.'"

This scriptural warning to pay attention to foundations and ultimately cost seems so directly aimed at church planters who are on the threshold of building a place to worship. I've heard it said that there are some people, good people, in the larger community who have watched the creation and development of All Saints' from a distance. They are fascinated and supportive of the unique role the church has in Benton County as a church that is open minded, inclusive, and diverse. However, they are reluctant to join All Saints' because they fear that, since we are a new church, membership will be costly. They are afraid that they will be asked to give mightily of their time, their energy, their talents, and their treasure.

In thinking of how I would respond to the reservations of these reluctant parishioners, I initially thought of assuring them that they can be as involved in the life of All Saints' as much, or as little, as they wished. And that is true. They may have taught Sunday school classes for twenty years, served on countless committees, been involved in outreach and worship and have grown tired of that kind of church work. I want to assure them that it's okay to let others do this kind of service. As for money, the rich and poor are equally welcome in our midst, and our parishioners give as they are able. An invitation to become an integral part of All Saints' is simply an invitation to be with us, to share in our journey of discovery.

But I also want to tell them that it is good for them, as it was for the man that intends to build a tower, to first sit down and estimate the cost. A decision to follow Jesus can be very costly. A decision to embrace our community, to allow the love of God to fully permeate a person's life, is to risk transformation.

What might that transformation cost? As Jesus said, "even life itself." Maybe old ways of living and being will have to be abandoned. Perhaps we will be compelled to let go of old prejudices. Discipleship moves us beyond familiar kinship ties and leads us into relationships within this body of fellow Jesus followers that would have never happened otherwise. You might find yourself waking up to a new reality and find that the way in which you have been operating in the world just doesn't work anymore. Awakening to who you are and to the life that God intends for you is the true cost of discipleship. Before we can build a tower, we have to first be clear about the nature of our discipleship.

Healing Water

From the bluff that overlooks Tiger Boulevard, which is where All Saints' will be built, a steep path descends to a small parcel of land on the north side of the road. A narrow stream that eventually becomes Sugar Creek winds its way through this thickly forested hollow. Several hundred yards to the southwest, the waters that form the creek emerge from deep within the earth at a red brick-lined spring called Park Springs. Over a century ago, a park was built there so that people from all around could benefit from its therapeutic, healing waters.

There is a point where the creek twists and turns, flows under a makeshift bridge, and then slows down as it forms a shallow pool lying beneath a jagged stone outcropping. A few industrious parishioners could stack a sufficient number of stones at the leading edge of the pool to delay the water's journey long enough to form a pool just deep enough for baptism. There, with Jesus present in the midst of the crowd, we could witness the baptismal candidates being healed and washed clean, not just with the clear, spring-fed waters of Sugar Creek, but with the presence of the Holy Spirit. The sacrament of baptism could take place in the midst of the wild, natural, tempest-filled world where the Holy Spirit likes to make her presence known.

I don't know if we will ever really hold baptisms in the waters of our spring-fed creek. It's a nice vision, but it doesn't really matter whether baptism takes place in the crystalline waters of a healing spring, in the muddy waters of the Jordan River, or in the sprinkling of warmed tap water that is made holy by God's people who seek God's blessing. What does matter is that we don't civilize things too much and that we don't refine the practice to the point that the wildness of the experience seeps away. We must always keep these sacramental practices sufficiently wild so that the Holy Spirit continues to be revealed to us.

We engage in the rite of holy baptism because it is part of our tradition. John the Baptist baptized in the Jordan River. Since then, millions of Christians have been initiated into the faith through the ritual reenactment of that fateful encounter between the Baptizer and the man named Jesus. However, we are not just a part of that great tradition. We are not merely descendants, but also ancestors. Those of us who gather for worship each week are taking part in the creation of the future of tradition. If people are still baptizing two thousand years from now, it's because people like us still find it important today.

Baptism is the beginning of a transformative experience. It is a symbolic movement into the earth beneath the waters of baptism. The water that splashes from the pitcher into the font and flows from a priest's hand onto a child's head is representative of the living waters necessary for us to grow into the fully realized human beings that we are meant to be. My prayer is that as we witness the waters of baptism nourish each newly born child, we may also be born anew ourselves. With the renewal of our baptismal vows, may we all be capable of experiencing the wild, unruly, and transformative presence of the Holy Spirit.

God Is Beauty

The 11/11/11 opening of the Crystal Bridges Museum of American Art and the inauguration of a design process that will culminate in the construction of a more permanent home for All Saints' Episcopal Church led me to ruminate on the nature of sacred space. The renowned Canadian Israeli architect Moshe Safdie designed a magnificent structure that is both a reflection of the natural landscape of Northwest Arkansas and a challenge to the aesthetic and spiritual sensibilities of its inhabitants. Crystal Bridges is a place of great beauty, where trails and waterways reach out and summon visitors to experience the transforming effect of the art that lies within the building. Through art, the visitors will come to know the creative force that lies within them as well.

Our physical environment forms us; our spiritual well-being is influenced by our surroundings. The natural world shapes us in very positive ways, teaches us to appreciate beauty, and provides us with moments of solitude amid the splendor of a mountain range or beside a spring-fed creek. Fifteen years ago, Benton County's villages contained little that was new. Walmart's worldwide success brought with it an unprecedented building boom. However, Benton County is still an architectural wasteland. Most of the public and private building that has taken place over the past decade has been soulless, a littering of ugly chain restaurants and nondescript office buildings, lying beneath a growing forest of electronic billboards. These are structures that could have been built anywhere and say nothing about our highest and best aspirations as a people.

The great contemplative Trappist monk Thomas Merton spoke of how we can become agents of truth and beauty, thus revealing the face of God. Merton said that "in the creation or contemplation of a work of art or a sacred space, an individual is raised above the mundane confines of his or her own needs and in that elevation—that exultation—can discover new horizons of thought, vision and moral action." We are becoming increasingly aware of our role as stewards of God's creation, making sure that streams flow free of pollutants, that the air remains fresh, that wooded hillsides are not left denuded and lifeless. But within our towns and cities we also have a responsibility to not only respect and care for God's created world, but to join with the divine as co-creators of an urban environment in which the intertwining of the spiritual and the physical can arise and uplift us.

The construction of Crystal Bridges holds great promise for the people of Bentonville. At the same time, the presence of such a building, with all its inherent benefits, presents us with a challenge. In conversation, I sense that people anticipate that the museum will change the community in ways that remain unclear at present. What the museum could provide is a threshold through which we may pass and emerge on the other side as a people with a new appreciation for beauty in all the fullness of the word. The museum could remain a remarkable singular achievement or it could establish a precedent for future construction in our city, calling on us to erect other buildings of similar stature. We could begin to ask of our city planners, architects, and builders, not simply to put up structures that meet our basic needs or enhance a corporate bottom line, but to create spaces that will house our hearts and lift our spirits. As we take pleasure in art and while we engage in the work of establishing more places of beauty and creativity we will be re-created as well.

In the church, we often refer to the sacraments as outward and visible signs of an inward and spiritual grace. In a city, art and architecture are the outward and visible signs of who the citizens are as a people, a reflection of their soulfulness. Sacred spaces do not reside solely within the churches, synagogues, and mosques of our community. At its best, art and architecture become mediators of the sacred, providing avenues through which a community can be brought closer to a spiritual core. The gift of Crystal Bridges represents a fine beginning. The creation of a sacred landscape that radiates beyond the museum's grounds and begins to tell us who we are will remain our collective responsibility.

Standing at the Threshold of the Holy

At All Saints', our architects and our congregation are in the midst of the conceptual design phase of the first Episcopal church to be built in Bentonville, Arkansas. Naturally, I'm spending a lot of time thinking about sacred space and how it can be intentionally created. As I write this morning, watching a thin layer of fog drift across the silent waters of Lake Avalon, the vapors rising in curls and then disappearing in the sun-warmed air, I marvel at our audacity and at the challenge we face in attempting to purposefully fabricate a place of transcendence when the natural world seems to effortlessly provide countless opportunities for humans to experience the holy.

I suppose my favorite church is Trinity Episcopal Church, which is located on the island of Maui. It is a small Episcopal church with exterior walls that only rise to a height of about three feet. The absence of a roof allows a Pacific breeze to carry the fragrance of the lokelani roses through the Sunday morning Eucharist. The sunlight, filtered through the branches and fronds of towering palms, provides the only warmth that is needed. The creators of this space seemed to recognize that their role was to get out of the way and allow the Creator to do her work of providing the experience of transcendence.

As nice as the weather can be in Arkansas, it's far from being a Hawaiian paradise and the winter climate requires that we work and worship indoors. Even the Maui church builders recognized the value of constructing a space that was set apart, designated for the purpose of acknowledging the presence of the Divine. But how can a church come close to replicating the sense of the Holy that nature readily provides?

Conversations with skilled architects are often about thresholds, the movement from one kind of space to another. The preliminary design for the entrance to our church calls for a wide, low-lying porch, with a dozen red doors that can be flung open on Sunday mornings, signaling to all that there is shelter and warm welcome within. Through the red doors, one passes into an interior garden, bringing the senses into play through the sights and smells of flora and fauna and the bubbling sounds of a baptismal pool. The passage toward the holy continues through the narthex, a gathering place where the welcoming carries on, but this time in the midst of sacred art that is carefully selected to remind visitors that their pilgrimage is in company of the saints. At particular times of the day, the narthex is traversed by a narrow beam of sunlight through which visitors will pass before finding themselves at the threshold of the nave, the principle worship space.

Within the nave, guests will be bathed in light, not directly from the sun, but filtered through a series of veils that allow shimmering light to enter inside and provide small glimpses of the surrounding meadow to remind us that while worship can't truly take place in isolation from the outside world, it is nonetheless possible to design particular places and moments in time so that, in those sacred locales, we are more likely to realize the presence of the transcendent.

In a sense, we are all standing at the threshold of the holy. The world abounds with the liminal, the transitions between one way of being and another or what the Celts call the "thin places." The congregation of All Saints' imagines a church building as a sacred space where particular attention is called to the state of the liminal; we are surrounded by opportunities to cross the threshold into the presence of the Divine. Nature presents the same occasion for transformation in every sunset and in every leaf that drifts across a still pond. You may arrive at a "thin place" by merely listening to the laughter of a child or hearing the prayer of the aged. We stand at the same threshold of change whenever we learn to love the unlovable and experience compassion in a new way.

Ultimately, it is a matter of expectation. When we enter into a space, a moment, or a situation with the anticipation of an encounter with the holy, God generally shows up. Even so, I'm compelled to wonder whether Mary and Joseph, as they walked together into the stable before welcoming the baby Jesus into the world, realized that they were passing through the threshold of the holy. Thomas

Merton writes, "Love laughs at the end of the world because Love is the door to eternity. He who loves is playing on the doorstep of eternity." Marcelo Gleiser, a physicist at Dartmouth College, looks for the sacred in his work on the edges of theoretical physics. He finds the sacred in "a place where you are not where you were before. A place where you have to pay attention." He describes the sensation of the sacred as "a feeling of awe with the mystery of what we do not know." For Gleiser, this is what makes science so compelling and why he regards his work as sacred. Science takes him to that which is unknown, into the presence of mystery, which is a sacred place.

Sometimes the Holy Spirit moves us in that direction, toward a place wherein we aren't altogether sure we are comfortable. It is a place of mystery, a place where we experience the unknown, and a place that expands our idea of what is blessed by God beyond the boundaries of what we had previously known.

Appendix: Practical Advice for the Church Planter

1. Make friends. Open yourself up to wide-ranging encounters. Start up conversations with strangers, but don't be pushy. You are looking for friends, not converts. At its early stages, planting a church is a little like a bunch of first dates.

2. Get involved in community life. Engage in whatever things interest you. If you have a child who plays baseball, coach the team. If you like to run, join the runners' club. If you like politics, attend city council meetings. You will meet people in the natural course of doing things you like to do.

3. Spend as little time as possible in your office. Do your work in local cafés, coffee houses, or the library. If you are a regular at a few places, people will reach out to you.

4. Wear your clerical collar everywhere. People will begin to recognize you and approach you. Be open to the conversations that the collar will inspire. People will be curious. Capitalize on that curiosity.

5. Get to know the reporter that covers the religion/lifestyle section of the local newspaper. They will call on you to comment on religious issues. If you are a good writer, write a column in the local paper. If you are bold in proclaiming

the gospel in print, you will reach far more people than you do from the pulpit.

6. Learn about the community where you now live. Read its history and stay current on events that are of local interest. Immerse yourself in the community.

7. Have a plan. Before you arrive in town, carefully outline the initial steps you will take to begin planting the church. Be willing to alter the plan as circumstances and the movement of Holy Spirit guide you.

8. Enlist help from those who share your vision. The friends that you are making will be of great help here. You can't start the church by yourself.

9. As you make friends, organize small group meetings: book studies, Bible studies, get-acquainted sessions, community service projects, parties, etc. Our "Theology Pub" is our longest lasting small group and has proven to be an excellent introduction to the church.

10. Offer something different. If you are in an area where many churches already exist, you must offer something that sets you apart from everyone else. Find a niche.

11. Approach establishing a church like it is a single project and move toward accomplishment of the goal. You are on a mission.

12. A startup church will attract people who have not been able to find a church elsewhere, for all kinds of reasons. Reach out to the margins, the disenfranchised, and the alienated. You may attract a fair number of misfits, but you will also attract a good number of more stable people who respect a church where everyone is welcomed. Be intentionally inclusive.

13. Move with all deliberate speed. Don't stop moving forward, but enjoy the experience all along. Each phase is interesting; embrace them all.

14. Hold off on offering Sunday services as long as you can. Wait an entire year if possible. If you start having Sunday services with a handful of people, there will be a tendency

to think of the church as a small congregation. That mentality will make it harder to grow.

15. Get to know some musicians. You will need them.

16. Love the people, even if they aren't always lovable. If they know that you love them, they will forgive your inadequacies.

17. Have a partner who respects and supports the work you are doing. Your partner should have his or her own passion, otherwise it will be difficult for them to accept your need to spend a lot of time engaging others.

18. Get married. Although you are frequently in the company of others, it's lonely work. Single clergy can also attract attention that will divert you from the mission.

19. Get a truck. You will be hauling a lot of stuff around. A pickup is very useful.

20. Fail fast and quit early. If a particular plan isn't working, be quick to recognize that and adjust tactics.

21. Pick a church plant location where the population is growing or shifting demographically. It is very difficult to change established patterns of church-going. If new people are moving into the community, they are more likely to take a look at what you are doing.

22. Put together a website that is more directed to those outside the church than within.

23. Extensively utilize social media, but do not imagine that the "virtual church" is a substitute for face-to-face interaction. It is too easy to spend all day on Facebook or Twitter and imagine that you are actually building substantial community.